NINJA PLANTS

SURVIVAL AND ADAPTATION
IN THE PLANT WORLD

WILEY BLEVINS

TWENTY-FIRST CENTURY BOOKS / MINNEAPOLIS

To Jerome Su, who inspired this book after our walk through the campus grounds of National Taiwan University in Taipei

A special thanks for technical support on the initial draft to botanist James Boyer, Vice President for Children's Education, New York Botanical Garden

Text copyright © 2017 by Wiley Blevins

Twenty-First Century Books
A division of Lerner Publishing Group, Inc.
241 First Avenue North
Minneapolis, MN 55401 USA

For reading levels and more information, look up this title at www.lernerbooks.com.

Main body text set in Bembo STD Regular 12/15.
Typeface provided by Monotype Typography.

Library of Congress Cataloging-in-Publication Data

Names: Blevins, Wiley, author.
Title: Ninja plants : survival and adaptation in the plant world / by Wiley Blevins.
Other titles: Survival and adaptation in the plant world
Description: Minneapolis : Twenty-First Century Books, [2016] | Includes bibliographical
   references and index. | Description based on print version record and CIP data provided by
   publisher; resource not viewed.
Identifiers: LCCN 2016021288 (print) | LCCN 2016018339 (ebook) | ISBN 9781512428537
   (eb pdf) | ISBN 9781512410136 (lb : alk. paper)
Subjects: LCSH: Plants—Adaptation—Juvenile literature.
Classification: LCC QK921 (print) | LCC QK921 .B54 2016 (ebook) | DDC 581.4/7—dc23

LC record available at https://lccn.loc.gov/2016021288

Manufactured in the United States of America
1-39561-21260-8/17/2016

CONTENTS

A SECRET, REMARKABLE WORLD

WHAT CAN COMMUNICATE BUT HAS NO MOUTH, CAN SMELL BUT HAS NO NOSE, AND CAN ATTACK BUT HAS NO HANDS?

The answer: a plant! When you think about plants, you might admire the beauty and sweet fragrance of flowers, appreciate the taste of fruits and vegetables, or think about the many products we get from wood, such as furniture or paper. But you might not realize that plants are far more complex than their beauty, taste, and utility in everyday life and that many are in a constant struggle with one another for survival. Every day, plants wage a fierce battle—a struggle for the best soil, the most direct sunlight, and domination of the land's resources. Unless we observe plants carefully, humans mostly miss these struggles, because they occur at a slow pace and almost silently.

Skunk cabbages emit a strong odor that attracts insects such as flies, bees, and beetles. The insects carry pollen between male and female parts of skunk cabbage flowers, helping the plants reproduce.

The scientific study of plants is called botany. Botanists observe, research, and record plant behavior, and plants certainly have some surprises for us. From plants that act aggressively—almost like ancient ninja warriors—to those that behave like secret agents and tricksters, the world of plants is as diverse and action-packed as it is fascinating.

Some plants, such as the stinking hellebore and the skunk cabbage, emit odors that are offensive to humans. But the odors attract the insects and animals that pollinate these plants as part of reproduction. Without pollination, these plants would become extinct. Other plants, such as the laughing bumblebee orchid, have evolved over many generations to resemble the insects they need to lure their way for pollination. The Venus flytrap, which grows in mineral-deficient soil,

Plants use various methods to disperse their seeds over a wide area. Some plants rely on the wind to blow seeds to new spots. The seeds sprout and grow in the soil where they land.

survives by being a carnivore (flesh eater), specifically by eating insects. This plant draws nitrogen and other vital minerals from the bodies of the insects and other small animals it devours. Lithops take the shape of pebbles to trick their plant-eating predators into passing them by.

Other plants lie dormant (inactive), appearing dead for periods of time, to survive harsh climates or to deceive hungry animals that might want to munch on their leaves. Parasitic plants, such as the strangler fig, are far more aggressive. They suck host plants to get the nutrients they need to live. They might also hog all the sunlight and water in the area. This sometimes results in the host plant's death. Plants also use botanical tricks to disperse their seeds over a wide area. For example, the spiny seedpods of burdock burrs grab onto animal and human passersby, who unknowingly carry the seeds with them to new spots, where they will sprout and grow. The seedpods of some fruit plants explode like mini bombs, shooting seeds over a wide area to ensure that new plants of the species will grow there.

You might have some of these sneaky, creepy, and sometimes violent plants in your own backyard. One or more of these plants might even be lurking in your home in a decorative pot. You might see some of these plants at a local park or community garden. They live in a world few people regularly notice, but this secret world of plants, with bizarre stories to tell, is waiting to be discovered.

EVOLUTION 101

Ukrainian American biologist Theodosius Dobzhansky once said, "Nothing in biology makes sense except in light of evolution." In evolution a species, or specific type of living thing, changes and adapts to its environment over many generations. Famed English naturalist Charles Darwin (1809–1882) was the first to describe the process of evolution, which he published in his landmark 1859 book *On the Origin of Species.*

A number of different processes can cause plant species to change. The most common is natural selection (living things pass on to their offspring beneficial traits that help them survive). With each successive generation, the favorable traits become more common, while plants with less favorable traits do not reproduce and therefore die out. Natural selection often begins with a mutation, or a random change, in a plant's genes. Genes are chemical structures made of deoxyribonucleic acid (DNA). They are in the cells of all living things, and they direct the growth, behavior, and reproduction of living organisms. Parents pass on their genes to the next generation. Suppose a mutation in a plant's genes results in a new flower color that is very appealing to pollinating insects. With more pollinators, the plant is more likely to reproduce than plants with a less attractive flower color. The plant will pass the appealing color to its offspring, which will later reproduce and continue to pass on the color. Eventually, more and more plants of the species will have the new flower color.

BINOMIAL NOMENCLATURE

Throughout history, numerous scientists have devised ways to classify and identify plants and animals. Some early classification systems included long descriptions of a plant's or animal's identifying characteristics, often resulting in long and cumbersome names. To streamline identification, eighteenth-century Swedish botanist Carolus Linnaeus (1707–1778) created a scientific naming system called binomial nomenclature. It consists of just a two-word name for each living thing. The system's name comes from the Greek words *bi* and *nomos* (two parts) and the Latin word *nomenclatura* (name calling).

In this system, each plant or animal is named by its genus (biological ranking) and its species (specific type within that ranking). For example, all roses belong to the genus *Rosa*. Within that group are dozens of different kinds of roses, distinguished by their species names. For instance, some scientific names for roses are *Rosa persica* (the barberry-leaved rose), *Rosa arkansana* (the prairie rose), and *Rosa rubiginosa* (the sweetbriar rose). In scientific writing, the genus in a plant's name is always capitalized, and both the genus and species names are italicized or underlined. The scientific name can be written out fully (for example, *Rosa arkansana*), or the genus name can be abbreviated using only the initial letter (*R. arkansana*).

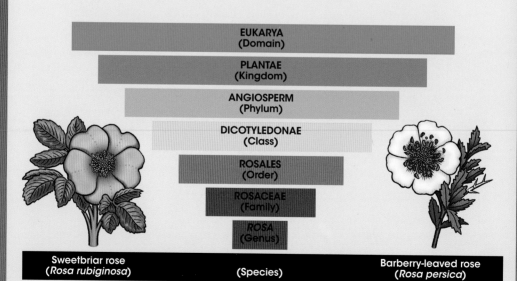

EUKARYA
(Domain)

PLANTAE
(Kingdom)

ANGIOSPERM
(Phylum)

DICOTYLEDONAE
(Class)

ROSALES
(Order)

ROSACEAE
(Family)

ROSA
(Genus)

Sweetbriar rose
(*Rosa rubiginosa*)

(Species)

Barberry-leaved rose
(*Rosa persica*)

Another evolutionary process is migration. During migration, wind and other natural forces carry plants (and their genes) to new areas. For example, a strong storm might carry sperm-bearing grains called pollen to a place many miles away. The sperm will fertilize plants in the new area. The resulting seeds will eventually sprout and become young plants. Because these plants carry genes from the far-off place mixed with genes from local plants, they will be genetically different from other local plants. New traits will appear in this new generation of plants.

Another evolutionary process is genetic drift. This is a random change in the genetic makeup of a population of living things. For example, suppose a rock slide wipes out most of the dominant plants in one area. With those plants gone, another kind of plant, from the same species but with a different genetic makeup, might take over and thrive. Plants with the old genetic traits will gradually disappear.

SURVIVAL MECHANISMS

Plants need light, minerals, water, and space to survive. Many plants have evolved to compete with other plants for the resources they need. This competition can occur underground, at the root level, where plants might struggle with one another to obtain the most water and minerals. Competition can also occur aboveground. For instance, plants might compete with one another for optimal sunlight, which is necessary for photosynthesis (plants using light to produce nutrients). Some plants even engage in allelopathy, a type of chemical warfare. They release toxic chemicals to poison the soil of neighboring plants, thereby reducing the number of plants competing with them for resources.

Other plants have developed defense mechanisms against the herbivores, or plant-eating animals, that threaten their survival. These defenses include sharp spikes or thorns that can puncture the skin of a predator. Or a plant may alter its appearance to resemble an inedible object that a predator won't view as a food source. Some plants emit ethylene gas, the smell of which wards off attackers.

LEAVES: NATURE'S BRILLIANT MODIFICATIONS

Leaves (*below*) are the food factories of plants. During photosynthesis, the green pigment chlorophyll (occurring naturally in a plant's leaves) absorbs carbon dioxide, water, and sunlight to create sugars. These, along with minerals from the soil, give plants the nutrients they need to live, grow, and reproduce.

For plants to carry out photosynthesis, they need lots of sunlight. That's why leaves come in many sizes. For example, in dense rain forests, many plants near the forest floor have oversized leaves. Because of the heavy canopy of trees overhead, very little sunlight penetrates to the rain forest floor. The big leaves help plants near the ground catch as much of the limited light as possible.

Leaves come in a variety of shapes too. For example, they may be round, oval, lobed, or sword-shaped. Some grow in rows, clusters, or pairs. Certain shapes probably evolved for certain reasons. For instance, sunlight can slip through the lobed upper leaves of ferns to reach lower leaves on the same plant.

In rain forests and other wet areas, some plants have leaves with pointy ends called drip tips. These allow excess rainwater to run off the leaves. This system keeps leaves mostly dry, so they can still respire (turn food into energy) during rainstorms and so they don't get moldy, which can be deadly for leaves.

Some plants have evolved to survive in harsh environments, such as those with extreme humidity, rainfall, or temperatures. For example, in extremely dry places, some plants lie dormant for days, months, or longer. They appear withered or dead but are actually conserving energy until more moisture is available. Then they will

Acacia trees have evolved to protect themselves from predators. Their sharp spines repel animals that might want to eat their leaves or bark. Some acacia trees also emit toxic chemicals from their leaves.

again become green and healthy looking. In extremely cold areas of the world, plants might grow low to the ground to avoid chilling winds or spread their roots along a thin top layer of soil because the soil underneath is frozen.

Symbiosis (a close and long-term interaction) between plants and other organisms is another survival mechanism. For example, some plants emit alluring odors or adopt attractive disguises to attract the birds and insects they need for pollination. Symbiosis can also take the form of mycorrhizae (intricate relationships between certain plants and fungi). In these situations, fungi colonize a plant's root system. The fungi share water and nutrients with the plant. In turn, the plant provides the fungi with some of the glucose it creates during photosynthesis.

PLANT REPRODUCTION

Plants, like all living things, must reproduce to continue their species. Some plants reproduce sexually, combining sperm (male reproductive cells) and eggs (female reproductive cells) to create a new life-form. Many flowering plants reproduce sexually. In the flowers, anthers (small saclike structures), which sit on the ends of stamens (stalks), produce pollen. This sticky powder gets its color from flavonoid compounds, which are responsible for plant pigmentation. While pollen can vary in color, it is usually yellow. The word *flavonoid* is derived from the Latin word *flavus*, meaning "yellow."

Pollen produces sperm. For a flowering plant to reproduce, pollen must move from the male portion of a flower (the stamen) to the female portion of the same flower (the pistil, style, and ovary) or to the female portion of another flower of the same species. When pollen reach a pistil, sperm from the pollen travel down a style, or tube, to the plant's ovary. In the ovary, sperm fertilize egg cells inside structures called ovules. After fertilization, ovules grow into seeds, and the ovary surrounding the ovules turns into fruit with one or more seeds. Fruits include everything from the peaches and apples you might find in a household fruit bowl to corn, tomatoes, peas, and beans.

Pollen doesn't move from the male part of the flower to the female part of the flower on its own. It moves with assistance of outside pollinators,

In flowering plants, fertilization takes place when pollen from a flower's male reproductive organs travels to a flower's female reproductive organs. Pollen vectors include insects, birds, and wind.

POLLINATION BETWEEN FLOWERING PLANTS OF THE SAME SPECIES

pollen grain (enlarged)

sperm cell

petal

pollen grain

stigma

style

pistil (female reproductive organs)

anther
filament

ovary

stamen (male reproductive organs)

ovules

pollen grain

The Pollination Process

1 Anthers produce pollen.

2 Pollen grains produce sperm.

3 A pollinator, such as an insect, bird, or wind, carries pollen to a flower's female portion.

4 Pollen reaches the stigma of another flower.

5 Sperm cells from the pollen move down the style to the ovary.

6 In the ovary, egg cells form inside ovules.

sperm cells

egg cells

withered style

fruit

seeds

sperm cells

7 Sperm cells unite with egg cells in the ovules.

8 The ovules become seeds.

9 The ovary develops into a fruit with seeds.

known as pollen vectors. Common biotic, or living, pollen vectors include bees, wasps, butterflies, moths, birds, bats, mosquitoes, and flies. For instance, bees and butterflies might land on the pollen-covered anther of a zinnia flower, attracted by its bright colors. Birds might dip their beaks into petunias and other tubular flowers to drink the sugar-rich nectar at the bottom. Some insects, such as honeybees, eat pollen itself. As birds and insects explore the flowers, grains of pollen from the anthers stick to the animals' bodies. As the animals move from flower to flower, some of the pollen on their bodies falls off onto pistils and begins fertilization.

Abiotic (nonliving) forces such as water and wind can also carry pollen from one flower to another. Abiotic pollination is common

This up-close photo of a white-tailed bumblebee on a flower shows yellow grains of pollen stuck to the bee's body. As the bee moves from flower to flower, some of the pollen will fall onto female flower parts, leading to fertilization.

among grasses, pine trees, and some palm trees. In some trees and shrubs, reproduction takes place in cones instead of flowers. The wind carries pollen from male cones (usually at the bottom of a tree or at the base of a branch and often growing in clusters) to female cones (usually at the top of a tree or at the tip of a branch), and fertilization takes place there. This positioning of the cones allows for easier fertilization, as pollen from the low-lying male cones drifts up with the wind to the higher-placed female cones on the same plant or to those on nearby trees. Seeds grow inside female cones, or seed cones.

Once seeds form inside a plant's fruit or cones, the reproductive journey continues. Seeds must be dispersed and embedded in soil so they can germinate (start to grow) and become new plants. Seeds are dispersed in different ways. For example, pulled by gravity, an apple might fall to the ground and break apart. Its seeds will grow in the soil where it falls. Other plants, such as dandelions and milkweed, have dry, light seeds that travel to new places by floating in the wind. Gorse is an example of a plant with a ballistic method of seed dispersal. Its seedpods explode, often as a result of heat, shooting seeds away from the parent plant. Sometimes animals devour tasty fruit and drop or spit out the seeds as they eat. Other times, animals eat seeds along with the rest of the fruit. When the animals defecate onto the ground, the seeds grow in the soil where they land. Other seeds stick to the fur and skin of passing humans and other animals, hitching a ride to a new location, where they will eventually drop to the soil and grow.

Many plants reproduce asexually, without the fertilization that brings male and female cells together. Asexual reproduction requires only one parent plant. The offspring are clones—genetically identical to the parent. In asexual reproduction, plant cells divide and make copies of themselves through mitosis. In one type of asexual reproduction, plants send out stolons (runners) along the surface of the soil. Where they touch the ground, nodes on stolons establish roots and grow into new plants. In another type of asexual reproduction, new buds sprout from underground plant structures, such as rhizomes, tubers, or bulbs.

AXEL ERLANDSON: PLANT SCULPTOR

Most plants developed their unique traits as a result of long-term evolutionary change. However, the growth patterns of some plants have been altered with assistance from humans. One California artist, Swedish-born Axel Erlandson (1884–1964), transformed trees into incredible works of art. His works are called arborsculpture—living trees that have been given a predetermined shape (such as a heart) or structure. People from all over the world have traveled to California to view Erlandson's "circus trees." Some of them are still living at Gilroy Gardens in Gilroy, California.

Erlandson sculpted the trees as they grew, redirecting their limbs through grafting. Grafting has been around for thousands of years and can be traced back to ancient China and the ancient Middle East. A form of asexual reproduction, grafting involves connecting sections of two different plants—usually of the same species—to form a single new plant. One section, called the scion, is a bud, branch, or piece of stem. The other section, called the rootstock, is the main stem or trunk of a plant, connected to the roots. Gardeners and farmers wedge these two parts tightly together, securing them in place with wax or paint. The plants' cambiums, or layers of tissue between the bark and the inner wood, eventually grow new cells and fuse the two parts into a single unit.

Axel Erlandson used grafting for aesthetics, to shape sections of trees to look like rings, baskets, lightning bolts, hearts, and other objects. Farmers use grafting to change a plant's characteristics, growing habits, or disease resistance, especially with crops such as apples, cherries, citrus trees, eggplants, and tomatoes. To do so, they graft a scion from a plant with desired characteristics to a rootstock of the plant they want to strengthen or change. This hybridizing (combining different species or types) creates new varieties or new species of plants.

In a process called arborsculpture, growers turn trees into works of art. This "basket tree" from Turkey was created by grafting, or fusing, several different trees together so that they grow as one.

The advantages of asexual reproduction include the ability to reproduce quickly, to reproduce without a mate or pollinator, and to reproduce in isolated areas with few pollinators.

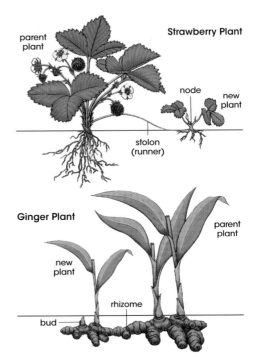

TWO TYPES OF ASEXUAL REPRODUCTION

Strawberry Plant

parent plant

node

new plant

stolon (runner)

Ginger Plant

parent plant

new plant

rhizome

bud

Strawberry plants send out long stems called stolons, or runners, along the surface of the soil. Where they touch the ground, nodes on the stolons can establish roots and grow into new plants (*top*). Ginger plants store starches and sugars in fleshy underground structures called rhizomes. Buds sprout from the upper surfaces of rhizomes, growing through the soil to become new plants (*bottom*).

PHOTOSYNTHESIS, RESPIRATION, AND TRANSPIRATION

Plants make their own food through photosynthesis. In this complex chemical process, occurring only in daylight, chlorophyll—a chemical pigment in green leaves—absorbs energy from sunlight. This energy combines with carbon dioxide and water from the air and soil to create photosynthates. They include sugars, starches, carbohydrates, and proteins. Plants use photosynthates, combined with minerals from the soil, to make the nutrients they need to survive. During photosynthesis, plants release oxygen as a waste product. The oxygen exits plants via their leaves and enters the atmosphere. Animals and humans breathe that oxygen, which they need to survive.

During respiration (similar to breathing), plants break down the nutrients they have created and turn them, along with oxygen, into

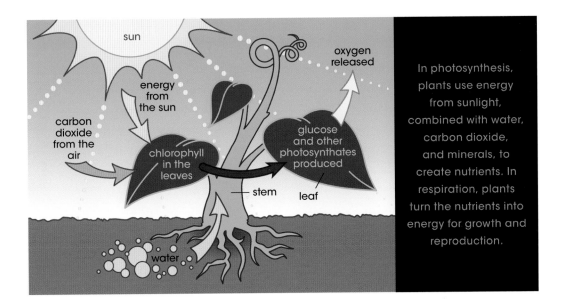

In photosynthesis, plants use energy from sunlight, combined with water, carbon dioxide, and minerals, to create nutrients. In respiration, plants turn the nutrients into energy for growth and reproduction.

energy for growth and reproduction. Respiration does not need sunlight. So it can take place day and night. Carbon dioxide and water are by-products of plant respiration.

In transpiration, water enters plants through their roots and travels to their stems, branches, and leaves. This water plays an important role in photosynthesis and plant cell growth. The water also carries essential minerals from the soil, such as phosphorus, potassium, and nitrogen, from the roots to the rest of the plant. It cools the plant as well.

In transpiration, water moves upward through a plant's stems and stalks. The water evaporates (turns into a gas called water vapor) when it reaches the plant's leaves. Evaporation creates a kind of suction, pulling on the water remaining in the plant, similar to sucking water through a straw. Transpiration speeds up when the surrounding air is dry, the wind is blowing, or the air temperature rises. These conditions lead to faster rates of evaporation, which causes the suction to increase.

MISSION CONTROL

While plants don't have brains like animals do, they do have phytohormones (plant hormones). These chemical substances control their growth and life cycles. Plant hormones occur in low concentrations, but they control everything from when a plant flowers to when buds form and where roots grow.

Plants have six main kinds of hormones: ethylene, cytokinins, auxins, gibberellins, abscisic acid, and brassinosteroids. Each plays a unique role in plant development. For example, some trees emit ethylene gas when fruit in one part of the tree begins to ripen. The gas signals fruit in other parts of the tree to ripen as well. The result is uniform ripening across the whole tree. This system is beneficial to trees that require animals for seed dispersal. A tree full of ripe fruit attracts animals, which spread seeds by either dropping or spitting them out while eating fruit or by defecating undigested seeds after eating fruit.

Cytokinins, found in a plant's roots, control cell division. These hormones determine which cells will turn into which plant parts. They also help trigger shoot formation. Auxins control a plant's tendency to grow shoots and stems upward instead of outward. Gibberellins affect stem and leaf growth. They kick in when the weather gets warmer and the days grow longer. For instance, gibberellins help lettuce leaves elongate in spring. They also regulate the growth of seeds, buds, and flowers. Abscisic acid helps regulate plant growth in a different way. For example, it can inhibit plant growth or can trigger bud dormancy. This protects plants during extreme conditions, such as cold winters or droughts. Brassinosteroids are steroid hormones that can increase plant yield and quality, similar to how steroids can build bigger muscles in humans.

GERM OF AN IDEA

The intricacies of plant reproduction, photosynthesis, respiration, and transpiration have evolved over millions of years. Plants have developed all sorts of tricks in their struggle to nourish themselves, repel predators, survive in harsh environments, and reproduce. Through observation and experimentation, botanists have discovered much about this secret, remarkable world of plants.

I became fascinated with plant survival tactics when I gave a speech to local teachers at National Taiwan University in Taipei. After my talk, a professor who is also an amateur botanist took me on a tour of the university grounds, which boast a large collection of plants and trees from around the world. Our first stop was a tree whose bark sported large spikes partway up its trunk to deter small animals from eating its bark. I had never seen anything like it. Our second stop was a tree with peel-away bark. This helps the tree survive devastating forest fires. As a child, my botanist guide would peel off bark from this kind of tree and use it as paper for writing and drawing. Our third stop was a plant whose leaves resembled an insect. Its appearance had evolved to attract other insects for pollination. I couldn't believe what I was seeing. I had never before learned about

Wiley Blevins was inspired by a visit to a garden in Taiwan. He loves gardens, such as this one too in New York's Central Park.

these fascinating plants, including the ways they sometimes fought one another for survival. Like ninjas—stealthy, fierce, and sometimes deadly—these plants were waging a war around me. It was a war I had never before noticed. During this tour, the idea for a book about the strange and intriguing world of plants began to sprout.

1

P.U., YOU STINK!

IMAGINE YOU ARE HIKING THROUGH A
TROPICAL FOREST WHEN SUDDENLY YOU GET A
BIG WHIFF OF SOMETHING NASTY.

You sniff under your arms. Not you. Then you lean over and sniff at your best friend because, let's face it, it really could be him. But alas, it's not your best friend either. What can be causing this offensive odor? It's the stinkiest, smelliest, most malodorous plant in the forest—the carrion flower. And you've just rubbed up against it. Ewww!

The titan arum (*Amorphophallus titanium*) is native to Sumatra, an island in Indonesia in Southeast Asia. This flower is also known as the carrion, or corpse, flower because it smells like the rotting flesh of a dead and decaying body. Although it looks like one, single flower, it is actually a cluster of flowers on a stalk, together called an inflorescence. The inflorescence's disgusting smell might prevent most animals from approaching the flowers to eat them—and will certainly keep away most sane people. Carrion flies and beetles, however, are attracted to the smell of rotting, dead animals, on which they lay their eggs. They can't race

The flower of the titan arum smells like a dead body, but flies and other bugs like the smell and swarm to the flower to lay their eggs there. In the process, they pollinate the flower.

to the titan arum fast enough! Like a ninja in disguise, the plant uses its odor to fool these insects into coming close. That's a good thing for the titan arum because as the bugs explore each flower, they are actually pollinating it—transferring pollen from the flower's male sex organ, the anther, to the female sex organ, the pistil.

The corpse flower isn't the only putrid-smelling plant in forests and gardens in Southeast Asia. If you travel throughout Indonesia, Malaysia, the Philippines, or Thailand, you might encounter the Rafflesia (*Rafflesia arnoldii*). The Rafflesia derives its name from Thomas Stamford Raffles (1781–1826) a British statesman-explorer

The Rafflesia doesn't have leaves to carry out photosynthesis. Instead, this parasitic plant latches onto a tropical grapevine and extracts nutrients from this host. The Rafflesia also smells like rotting meat, an odor that entices insect pollinators.

and the founder of modern Singapore, once a British trading post. The flower of this rare and exotic species smells like rotten flesh, so it's easy for pollinators to find it in the forest. The Rafflesia, often called the stinking corpse lily, produces the largest flower in the world—as big as 40 inches (102 centimeters) in diameter. That's more than 3 feet (1 meter) across! The plant's beautiful orange flower usually opens for only four days a year and then shrivels into a black, slimy mess. The horrid smell it emits attracts carrion flies. When the flower is in bloom, flies move around inside it, collecting its sticky and gooey pollen on their bodies. In this way, they transfer pollen between male and female parts of the flower, enabling fertilization.

Another unusual feature of the Rafflesia is that it has no leaves or stems. It grows low to the ground, attaching itself to and burrowing inside the tropical grapevine *Tetrastigma*. The only part of the Rafflesia that is visible outside of the host vine is its giant five-petaled flower. Why does the Rafflesia attach itself to the vine in the first place? Without green leaves, the Rafflesia cannot produce its own food through photosynthesis. Instead, it must live as a parasite on the host grapevine. Then the Rafflesia obtains all its nutrients from the vine it grows on.

The dead horse arum (*Helicodiceros muscivorus*), native to the stony islands of Corsica and Sardinia in the Mediterranean Sea, also smells like rotting flesh. And yes, the smell is the plant's way of attracting flies—in this case blowflies—for pollination. This plant can do something else extraordinary: it can raise its body temperature. That's right, this plant has a built-in heating system! The ability to grow warm (thermogenesis) is rare among plants, but it is part of respiration. The dead horse arum's warmth, along with its stench, attracts flies to its flower.

Blowflies are critical to the plant's fertilization, which isn't as simple as you might think. Each dead horse arum flower has only a two-day window of opportunity for pollination. The female part of each flower can receive pollen for only one day, but on that day, the male part is not mature enough to release pollen. On the following day, when the male part can release pollen, the female part has already withered. That's where the blowflies come in. The dead horse arum emits its characteristic horrid odor to attract blowflies for pollination at just the right time. On day one, the flies explore the plant's flower, looking for a place to lay their eggs. When they reach the female portions of the flower, spines in the floral chamber trap the insects inside, holding them overnight. During this time, the flies release pollen picked up from earlier visits to other flowers. The next day, the spines wilt and the flies are able to exit the chamber. As they leave, they pass by the male part of the flower, which on this day is ready to release pollen. The blowflies get covered in more pollen and fly off to pollinate more female flowers. The one-day delay is perfect timing for the dead horse arum.

A VARIETY OF STINKY SMELLS

Not all plants that stink smell alike. The skunk cabbage (*Symplocarpus foetidus*), common to North America and Asia, has a smell that fits its descriptive common name. If you crush the leaves of this plant, the odor is more like a skunk's nasty spray than a fresh spring breeze. The plant also emits this smell when its flower blooms. The smell attracts pollinators such as flies, bees, and carrion beetles. This symbiotic arrangement, in which the plant relies on insects for fertilization and the insects benefit from drinking the plant's nutrient-rich nectar, is a common evolutionary adaptation in plants. The plant's smell and the burning sensation from eating the plant or coming in contact with its broken stems is a defense mechanism that wards off larger animals that might damage or eat the plant.

The skunk cabbage has something else in common with the dead horse arum—it gives off heat through thermogenesis. In fact, its internal temperature can be up to 36°F (20°C) warmer than the outside air. What is this heat for? In winter the extra heat the skunk cabbage generates melts the snow and thaws out the frozen ground surrounding the plant. When the ground thaws, skunk cabbage seeds sprout and begin to grow. This is a competitive advantage in the plant world. It gives the skunk cabbage a jump start for spring. The early-sprouting skunk cabbage plant grabs the best nutrients in the surrounding soil, loads of extra sunshine, and more insects for pollination than other nearby plants. As they say, the early bird gets the worm!

The stinking hellebore (*Helleborus foetidus*), native to central and southern Europe, is another plant that lives up to its odorific name. The plant's lime-green flowers are beloved features in floral arrangements, and the plant doesn't normally have a pungent odor. However, its leaves react like those of the skunk cabbage under one specific condition. If the leaves are crushed, such as when an animal steps on the plant, the contact activates a surprisingly strong odor. This skunky smell is a great defensive adaptation to ward off predator animals. However, that's only one of the plant's ninja-like tricks. Yeast organisms inside the plant's nectaries (glands in the ovaries) can raise the temperature of the plant, which releases odiferous chemicals that attract pollinators.

HOT STUFF

The term *thermogenesis* is derived from two Greek words: *thermos* (hot, or heat) and *genesis* (origin, or creation). During thermogenesis, some living organisms create the heat they need for survival. Humans, for example, shiver, forcing their muscles to expend energy and create heat. In plants, thermogenesis has different purposes. The dead horse arum generates heat to create the smell that attracts pollinators. The skunk cabbage generates heat to warm up the soil around it so that its seeds will sprout in the early spring.

The dwarf mistletoe is a parasitic plant that lives on the bark of lodgepole pine trees in North America. As the mistletoe's seeds mature, they heat up. This heat causes the plant's fruit to explode at speeds of 60 miles (97 kilometers) an hour, shooting seeds as far away as 30 feet (9 m). The flying seeds are covered in a sticky substance that helps them adhere to lodgepole pine needles. When rain falls, the seeds slide from a tree's needles onto its twigs, germinate, and set up root systems in the tree's bark. A new dwarf mistletoe then grows on the bark as a parasite of the tree. This system ensures that the dwarf mistletoe species survives, although the plant eventually kills the host trees. In the United States, the US Department of Agriculture is trying to control the spread of dwarf mistletoe because of the damage it causes to lodgepole pines.

Just because a plant smells disagreeable doesn't mean the plant is ugly or unappealing. In fact, some plants that smell disgusting are quite attractive. If you were to stumble upon the white plume grevillea (*Grevillea leucopteris*) in Australia, you might be distracted by the beautiful yellow-white blooms of its flowers. But don't be fooled. Get close and you'll discover that this wily shrub's flowers smell like dirty socks. In fact, the white plume grevillea's nickname is Old Socks. Maybe this plant would be more at home in your school's gymnasium.

Another smell-o-rific organism is one of the smallest. It is the stinkhorn (family Phallaceae), which is common in tropical regions.

Stinkhorns and other mushrooms reproduce by releasing millions of tiny spores, which will grow into new organisms. Like many plants, stinkhorns attract flies (but repel humans) with their strong odor. The flies help spread stinkhorn spores to new locales.

You might not even notice it if you walked in the forest, but you can guess how it got its name! The stinkhorn isn't actually a plant. It is a mushroom (a type of fungus), an organism that obtains its food by absorbing nutrients from the living and dead plants and animals on which it lives. Stinkhorns are covered with smelly and sticky reproductive cells called spores, which stink like human waste. This smell is perfect for attracting carrion flies, which are crazy about the scent. The flies land on the brown slime covering the mushroom and devour the tasty sugars it contains. As they do, the mushroom's spores enter their digestive systems and also stick to their bodies. When the flies land elsewhere in the forest, they transfer the sticky spores through their feet and their feces, thereby dispersing the spores widely and allowing for more stinkhorns to grow and thrive.

FUNKY FRUIT

Asia, with its wealth of rain forests and diverse ecosystems, is home to some of the most fascinating plants in the world and has more smelly plants than most places. Perhaps the most popular of these plants is the durian tree (*Durio zibethinus*), which is common to

Indonesia, Malaysia, and Brunei. Known as the king of fruits, the durian has a foul smell, described by some as similar to rotten onions, decaying fish, or a sewer. Despite the smell, many people love the fruit for its delectable flavor. But this is not a unanimous opinion. Some people can't get past the smell to even try tasting it. In Malaysia, Singapore, and other Southeast Asian countries, eating the fruit in public is actually illegal because the disagreeable smell might upset the stomachs of people nearby.

An orangutan in Borneo, an island in Southeast Asia, feasts on the fruit of the durian tree. Orangutans and other animals aren't put off by the fruit's foul smell. The animals help the tree by spreading undigested durian seeds when they defecate.

Rather than attracting pollinators, the durian fruit's smell is part of a larger system of seed dispersal. In a symbiotic adaptation, large animals, such as pigs, orangutans, elephants, and tigers regularly dine on the fruit. The smell doesn't turn the animals off. It simply alerts them to the fruit's location and ripeness. When the animals defecate, they release any undigested durian seeds onto the ground. The seeds sprout and eventually grow into more durian trees.

2

FEED ME

WALKING THROUGH A FOREST CAN BE A
MINDFUL, PLEASANT EXPERIENCE, ALTHOUGH
OCCASIONALLY A NERVOUS HIKER WORRIES
ABOUT BEING ATTACKED BY A GRIZZLY BEAR OR
AN ANGRY MOUNTAIN LION.

However, no one ever worries about being devoured by a plant. But did you know that some plants are carnivorous? They eat meat!

Earth is home to nearly seven hundred species of carnivorous plants. Some of these plants live in harsh environments such as bogs and wetlands, where mineral-rich soil is limited. Others live in rocky areas, where it's difficult for plant roots to penetrate the soil. Plants in these areas are forced to look for nutrients elsewhere. So they have developed the ability to trap, eat, and digest insects and other small animals, including flies, ants, spiders, snails, and crickets. The plants mostly eat insects, which provide nutrients such as nitrogen and phosphorus, so botanists call them insectivorous plants. However, some plants do eat larger animals, such as frogs. But you can relax—the plants don't eat people.

All insectivorous plants use traps to capture their prey. Some use active traps, with portions of the plant actively and rapidly snapping shut or sucking in insects. Other plants use passive traps. They don't

Attracted by the fragrance and red interior of a Venus flytrap leaf, a fly has landed there to search for nectar. The leaf will soon snap shut, trapping the fly inside. The plant will then extract vital nitrogen from the fly's body.

involve movement by the plants. Instead, insects get trapped inside the plant on slippery inside walls or in sticky substances and cannot escape.

BUGS BEWARE!

The most well-known insectivorous plant is the Venus flytrap (*Dionaea muscipula*). It is native to the sandy bogs of North and South Carolina in the United States. Although this plant carries out photosynthesis to get much of the nourishment it needs, the soil there is low in nitrogen. So the Venus flytrap eats insects to get this vital nutrient.

The leaves of the Venus flytrap secrete fragrant nectar that attracts insects. The red color inside the plant's leaves also lures insects. Color is an attention grabber for pollinators, and different colors attract different insects and animals. For example, butterflies prefer bright colors such as orange, yellow, and red. Bees are most attracted to bright blue and violet. Hummingbirds prefer red or purple. The vibrant red of the inside of the Venus flytrap's leaves is like a flashing advertisement that shouts to certain insects, "Come, enjoy my nectar!"

But bugs beware. Once an insect lands inside the plant's leaves for a tasty treat, hairlike fingers along the leaves grab it. The leaves and fingers together form a snap trap that quickly shuts. The insects themselves become the tasty treat. For the trap to shut, an insect must touch the plant's hairs twice within twenty seconds. This response to touch or vibrations in plants is known as thigmonasty. Once the insect is trapped, the plant's leaves expel chemical enzymes, similar to the digestive juices that break down food in the human stomach. The enzymes dissolve the soft parts of the insect's body, extracting nutrients—mostly nitrogen—that help nourish the plant. It can take up to twelve days for a Venus flytrap to consume nutrients from an insect. After all the nutrients are extracted, the trap opens and releases the insect's exoskeleton, or outer shell.

DINNER IS SERVED

Welcome to the insectivorous bladderwort family. Like Venus flytraps, bladderworts employ active traps to catch insects. More than two hundred species of bladderworts (*Utricularia*) live on Earth. These small plants thrive in freshwater lakes and bogs. The plants' genus name comes from the tiny utricles (bubble-like bladders) on their leaves. The bladders are 0.5 inches (1.2 cm) across or smaller. When the plants photosynthesize, they require other nutrients that are not available in the acidic soil and water where they live. So they turn to the insect world for extra nutrition.

Whether they live in ponds, lakes, or bogs, bladderworts are surrounded by water. To lure unsuspecting water insects or tadpoles, bladderworts secrete sweet nectar through membranes that cover one end of each bladder. When an insect makes contact with sensitive hairs surrounding the membrane, water around the plant rushes into the bladder, sucking the animal in with it. The swirl of water pushes the bladder closed, trapping the insect in less than a second. It's the fastest-acting plant in the world. Over a period of hours or even days, the plant's digestive enzymes dissolve the soft parts of the animal. Bladderworts do not eat animals just to make up for mineral deficiencies. They also eat predator insects that might want to eat them—an important defensive behavior.

Like bladderworts, pitcher plants rely on insects for vital nutrients. The more than sixty different species of pitcher plants belong to a number of different genuses. All the plants have flutes, or pitcher-shaped leaves. The pitcher varies with each species. Some are shaped like beakers. Others

Pitcher plants mostly eat flies and other insects. But sometimes a frog falls into a slippery pitcher plant and lands in the digestive juices at the bottom. Unable to climb back out, the frog becomes the plant's next meal.

resemble narrow-necked wine bottles; tall, thin champagne glasses; or small lamps. The flutes are pitfall traps. Flies and other insects enter the flutes, attracted by their color and by the smell of a sweet nectar secreted by the pitchers. While it's easy for an insect to get into a flute, it can be hard to get out because the insides of flutes are slippery. Unable to leave the trap, the insect eventually drowns in digestive enzymes at the bottom.

A CLOSE CALL

Some non-insect-eating plants attract bugs in ways similar to those of insect-eating plants. The plants want the insects not to eat them but to help with pollination. Birthworts (*Aristolochia*) are one example. They live in diverse ecosystems around the world. Also known as Dutchman's pipes, the plants are woody climbing vines that produce flowers resembling pipes. The plants attract carrion flies and other insects with the strong smell of rotting meat. Their sticky flowers trap the insects that land there. But a birthwort doesn't consume these insects. It traps them only long enough to cover them with pollen. Once that happens, the sticky hairs shrink and release the insects. Then they go on to pollinate other birthworts. Talk about a close call!

The flying duck orchid (*Caleana major*) also catches and releases insects for pollination. To our human eyes, the reddish-brown flower of this Australian plant looks like a duck in flight. But male sawflies, attracted by chemicals released from the reproductive glands of the flower, think the flower is actually a female sawfly. When a male sawfly lands on the flower, the plant senses its weight and movement. In response, a tonguelike section of the flower called a labellum snaps down on the fly, trapping it inside the flower. This is another example of thigmonasty. The male sawfly, looking to mate with a female sawfly, tries to have sex with the flower, engaging in pseudocopulation (false sex). Meanwhile, pollen that had stuck to the fly during previous visits to other orchids is deposited to help fertilize the flower. The fly picks up even more pollen before breaking free from the trap and moving on to pollinate more orchids.

The flying duck orchid resembles a duck in flight. But because of its scent, male sawflies think the flower is a female sawfly. While the male fly tries to mate with the flower, the flower traps the fly briefly—just long enough for the fly to pick up and drop pollen for fertilization.

A sundew has trapped a common blue damselfly with the sticky structures on its leaves. Nitrogen and phosphorus from the bug's body will provide nourishment to the plant.

If you were to cut open the flute of a pitcher plant, you might find a mass of partially digested flies inside. The plant takes as much nourishment as it needs from the insects it traps, and the undigested portions simply remain inside the pitcher. Some pitcher plants eat even larger animals. In the United States, the trumpet pitcher sometimes eats small frogs that enter its flute. The frogs hide there to catch and eat unsuspecting insects lured to the plant, but then the frogs themselves become the plant's prey. One pitcher plant was found with a partially digested mouse inside. Others have eaten small birds.

STICKY SITUATIONS

Sundews (*Drosera*) grow in nutrient-poor conditions on every continent except Antarctica. Their leaves are covered with what look like glistening, droplet-shaped structures on the ends of tiny hairs. But these droplets, with their sweet smell and taste, are actually an effective trick for catching insects. When small flies and other insects land on the leaves, they stick to the droplets. As the insects struggle to get away, they touch other hairs with more sticky droplets. The leaves sense this struggle via thigmonasty, and they slowly roll inward, further trapping the bugs. The sticky droplets contain digestive enzymes that immediately go to work on the insects' bodies. The enzymes dissolve the insects, and the plant absorbs the nitrogen and phosphorus found in the insects' soft tissues.

Sundews are beautiful plants and do not look dangerous at all. With their small violet leaves, butterworts (*Pinguicula*) don't look dangerous either. But looks can be deceiving. The leaves of these insectivorous plants ooze a sticky, waterlike substance called mucilage. Fruit flies and gnats land on the leaves, believing the droplets are water. Once a bug has landed, the sticky goo traps the insect and releases enzymes to begin digesting it. The plant absorbs the nitrogen and phosphorus contained in the insect's insides, like a vampire sucking out its victim's blood. All that remains is the insect's empty carcass, or shell, which eventually falls off the leaf when the wind blows.

ONE TRICKY COBRA

Native to Northern California and southern Oregon, the cobra lily (*Darlingtonia californica*) has ominous-looking leaves. They take the form of bent tubes resembling the heads of cobras ready to attack. Even more ominous, two fanglike structures hang from each cobra head leaf. The leaves emit a sweet scent that attracts insects. They crawl into the tube searching for food and inevitably enter the tube's lower chamber. The insects, looking to escape, see what appear to be small windows of light at the top of the tube. However, these fenestrations, or false windows, are actually thin parts of the leaf that allow some light in but aren't legitimate exits. The insects, desperate to escape, beat their heads against the fenestrations until they tire, weaken, and fall back down the slippery sides of the tube. At the bottom, their

The cobra lily gets its name from its resemblance to the deadly snake. The plant itself is deadly to insects that crawl into its tube-shaped leaves looking for nectar. Unable to escape, the bugs end up at the bottom of the tube, dissolved by the plant's digestive enzymes.

trouble continues. When the insects attempt to climb out, sharp downward hairs prevent their escape. Exhausted, the insects eventually collapse to the very bottom of the tube, which is filled with digestive enzymes. Symbiotic organisms, such as certain types of bacteria, help the plant digest the insects. The bottom of the tube is the insects' final resting place. The plant itself thrives on nitrogen and phosphorus extracted from the insects' soft inner parts.

READY FOR BATTLE

SUPERSPY JAMES BOND HAS MANY GADGETS TO
PROTECT HIMSELF FROM VILLAINS: PENS WITH EXPLOSIVE
CHARGES, SHOES WITH HIDDEN DAGGERS, A ROCKET
BELT TO LAUNCH HIM AWAY FROM ATTACKERS, AND
EVEN NINJA STARS, OR THROWING STARS.

Some plants use similar weapons and techniques, including poisons,
spikes, and strangulation. Some weapons help plants protect themselves
from predators that might want to eat their leaves or bark. Others
keep plants from getting trampled. These weapons might not look like
traditional war tools, but they are just as effective. From exploding,
poisonous fruit to threatening spikes, these are plant defenses you
definitely don't want to mess with.

SPIKES AND THORNS (SCRATCH . . . RIP!)

The red silk-cotton tree (*Bombax ceiba*), found in China and nations of
Southeast Asia, is one of many plants with a built-in weapons system.

The holly plant has several layers of defense. First, its prickly leaves repel predators. Its berries are also mildly toxic to some large animals, including humans.

The tree is tall and straight, with beautiful red flowers. The fruits and flowers are found high up in the tree. In spring the tree's seed capsules explode, releasing white cottony fibers. Starting at ground level, conical spikes grow around the tree's trunk. The spikes keep animals from eating the tree's cambium, a layer of nutrient-rich tissue between the bark and inner wood that is essential for tree survival. The spikes are a very effective defensive mechanism.

Another plant with prickly defenses is the holly (*Ilex*), which is native to both temperate and subtropical regions of the world. Some of the plant's leaves are completely smooth. Some have a few sharp edges. And some are completely surrounded by prickly points. The prickliest leaves tend to grow lowest on the holly plant, as a defense against nonflying animals. While birds can use their beaks to eat the plant's red berries without harm from the sharp leaves, many larger animals, such as deer and goats, stay away from the berries, repelled by the leaves' thorny edges. What if an animal does manage to eat the plant's delicious-looking berries? The berries are mildly toxic to many large animals and to humans, causing diarrhea and vomiting.

Hawthorn trees (*Crataegus monogyna*) are native to Europe and parts of Africa and Asia and can grow in many other temperate climates around the globe. The trees have thorny twigs for defense. But these spikes, which grow up to 5 inches (13 cm) long, can't compare to those of rattan palm trees. Native to tropical forests of Africa, Asia, and Australia, these plants grow needles that measure up to 1 foot (0.3 m) long. That sounds like a superlong doctor's needle in a sci-fi movie! The rattan, a climbing vine, grabs onto neighboring trees with these spikes as it grows upward from the forest floor toward the sunlight. The buffalo acacia (*Acacia phlebophylla*), native to Australia, has similarly long and sharp thorns. Any animals and humans coming in contact with them will be severely scratched.

POISONOUS PLANTS (BEWARE!)

Many plants take a different approach to defense: they emit toxic gases or release harmful chemicals into the air. For example, various species of the acacia tree use chemicals to keep predators from eating their leaves. When large mammals such as antelope, cattle, and giraffes threaten, acacia leaves emit toxic chemicals called tannins. At the same time, the tree gives off the gas ethylene. Other trees in the vicinity detect the gas, alerting them to the predator danger. That's right—the plants smell one another. Then the other acacias start to emit ethylene gas. In some acacia species, the ethylene gas increases the toxicity levels in the plants' leaves. In other species, the tannin-filled leaves begin to droop. Animals sense the change and keep their distance.

Another plant that uses chemical signals to ward off predators is the willow tree (*Salix*). If a leaf-eating insect attacks the tree, it will emit an aspirin-like chemical, a derivative of salicylic acid, to repel the bug. Wild lima beans (*Phaseolus lunatus*) are even sneakier.

THE POISON GARDEN

"These Plants Can Kill." That's the warning sign on the imposing black iron gates (*below*) of Alnwick Garden in England. All the same, more than 350,000 visitors flock to Alnwick and its majestic castle each year to view the exotic and deadly plants. The visitors take a carefully monitored guided tour and are forbidden to touch any of the deadly plants. And deadly they are. The garden contains about one hundred lethal plants producing poisons such as hemlock, ricin, and strychnine. The garden also grows plants such as opium poppies (the source of heroin) and cannabis (the source of marijuana) to educate visitors on the mind-altering drugs derived from these plants.

When beetles start to eat this plant, it releases a chemical that attracts beetle-eating spiders and insects. They respond to the food-finding alert, and the beetles become a nutritious meal for these bugs. The beetles are eaten, and the wild lima beans survive the attack. The common tomato does something similar. When a caterpillar starts munching on its leaves, the tomato emits a chemical that summons a type of parasitic wasp. This is the plant's version of dialing 9-1-1. The wasps lay their eggs on the caterpillars, and the wasp larvae (newly hatched offspring) eat the caterpillars. How do plants know which insects are attacking them? Scientists believe that plants detect and identify certain digestive juices in the insects' oral secretions.

One of the deadliest and most feared poisons in nature is cyanide. In modern history, some captured war criminals have swallowed cyanide capsules to commit suicide rather than face trial and punishment for their crimes. The bracken fern (*Pteridium*), which grows on all continents except Antarctica, is one of many plants that produces cyanide in its leaves. Yep—poison leaves. Insects smell the lethal poison and won't even approach the plant. If an animal accidentally munches on this fern, the toxin can lead to blindness or cancer. Even so, some animals, such as horses and cattle, will eat the deadly fern when no other food is available. People in China, Japan, and Korea also eat the young stems of this fern, which are tasty, even though doing so has been linked to stomach cancer.

One of the most nightmarish toxic plants for humans is the giant hogweed (*Heracleum mantegazzianum*), a member of the parsley family. Hogweed can grow to be 15 feet (4.5 m) tall. This plant, common in central Asia, doesn't poison people or animals that eat it. Instead, it harms the skin. The plant's sap contains toxic chemicals called furanocoumarins, which are sensitive to light. If the sap gets onto human or animal skin that is then exposed to sunlight, the skin will begin to blister and burn. Ow-wee! The burn can lead to necrosis (the death of cell tissues) and huge purple lesions that can remain on the skin for years. If the toxins come in contact with the eyes, temporary blindness can follow. Hogs are immune to the plant's toxins, however.

The slobber weed (*Pilocarpus pennatifolius*), with its drippy common name, can make even the most elegant of us drool uncontrollably if we eat the plant. Although not toxic, a chemical in the weed sends a signal to the human or animal nervous system to overproduce saliva. If that isn't bad enough, the drooling is often followed by dizziness, nausea, and other unpleasant sensations.

STINGING PLANTS

The stinging tree (*Dendrocnide moroides*) of Australian rain forests (also known as the gympie-gympie tree) lives up to its painful name. The stinging tree is a type of nettle, a plant family characterized by leaves covered with stinging hairs (although not all nettles sting). The hairs are an important defense against predators. Although the stinging tree is frequently called the most dangerous plant in the world, you wouldn't know that by looking at its clusters of red fruit, which resemble bunches of delicious raspberries. But be warned. The plant's tiny hairs contain a neurotoxin known as moroidin. Just brushing up against the plant can cause the lethal hairs to embed in the skin. Once stung, a victim will experience unbearable pain. As Australian ecologist Marina Hurley said, "Being stung is the worst kind of pain imaginable—like being burnt with hot acid and electrocuted at the same time." Even worse, the pain can last for a year or more. In the worst cases, people go into anaphylactic shock after being stung, have heart attacks, and die. Botanists tell stories—which may or may not be true—of people who have had unfortunate encounters with this plant. One story tells of a man who accidentally fell on the plant. His pain grew so intense that he had to be tied to a hospital bed for three weeks. Another legend tells of a man in the Australian wilderness who mistakenly used leaves of the stinging tree as toilet paper. Uh-oh. The story says that his pain became so unbearable that he shot himself.

Another type of stinging nettle, found in the Amazon rain forest of Ecuador, causes pain but not as much harm as the stinging tree. The local Shuar people have been known to use the stinging leaves of this tree to punish their misbehaving kids. These kids would probably prefer detention.

EXPLODING PLANTS (DUCK FAST!)

Ancient ninjas made soft-cased bombs that released smoke and poison gas. Ninjas used these weapons to poison and temporarily blind their enemies. Some plants rely on explosions as well, and they do so to ward off predators or to disperse seeds. The sandbox tree (*Hura crepitans*),

The sandbox tree repels predators with its sharp spines, toxic sap, and poisonous fruit. When its fruits ripen, they pop open with a bang, hurling seeds several hundred feet in all directions.

common to tropical regions in North, Central, and South America, is a giant tree with huge leaves, beautiful red conical flowers, and sharp spines covering the trunk. The spines keep monkeys from climbing the tree, an important defensive behavior. The tree's sap is also toxic. In fact, indigenous hunters once put the sap on the tips of spears to kill fish and on the tips of hunting arrows to kill large game animals. But the truly frightening thing about this tree is its exploding poisonous fruit. That's right, its fruits are like mini bombs. When the fruits are ripe, they pop open with a loud bang. The explosion can hurl the poisonous seeds up to 300 feet (91 m) away at speeds of up to 160 miles (276 km) per hour. The fruit doesn't explode to scare off predators. It explodes to disperse its seeds. Why? Sandbox trees need to be spaced widely apart, so that each tree has enough room and can get enough nutrients to grow and thrive. So the tree needs to disperse its seeds widely for the species' survival. Once the seeds are dispersed, animals won't eat them because they smell the poison. Since the seeds aren't eaten, new plants have an increased chance of growing where the seeds fall.

The squirting cucumber (*Ecballium elaterium*), native to Europe, North Africa, and parts of Asia, also has an explosive nature. But unlike the yummy cucumbers in salads, squirting cucumbers are anything but tasty. People who mistakenly eat the fruit or any other part of the plant experience violent vomiting. Not only are the cucumbers poisonous, but when the fruits ripen, they burst open and with a hissing noise spray slimy mucilaginous liquid and black seeds up to 20 feet (6 m) away. The force of the explosion rips the fruit off the stalk. Stand clear! The juices can sting skin on contact.

A SLOW DEATH

The strangler fig (*Ficus aurea*), native to tropical habitats such as Florida and parts of the Caribbean islands, Mexico, and Central America, can be a killer plant. It grows in dense rain forests, where plants are forced to fight one another for light. Birds munching on the figs drop seeds on other trees as they fly away. The fig seeds germinate on the branches of the trees on which they land. Many seeds can germinate on one tree.

As the parasitic fig grows, it twists and tangles around the host tree, growing downward toward the ground. At the same time, it extracts nutrients from the host tree. The strangler also steals light from the host tree, and its roots hog the host's water. The host tree often dies.

It's easy to see how the strangler fig got its name. This parasitic plant wraps itself around host trees, stealing their nutrients, light, and water. Drained of vital resources, many hosts die.

4

COPYCATS

HALLOWEEN IS A NIGHT FOR DRESSING UP, PUTTING ON A MASK, AND ADOPTING A NEW PERSONA.

While roaming the streets on this spooky night, you might encounter people disguised as ghosts or black-clad ninjas, ominously slinking down the darkened streets. For one special night, those celebrating get to mimic somebody else. Some plants are also great mimics, but they don't do it for fun. They do it to increase their chances of survival. Plants, especially flowers, mimic other life-forms in a variety of ways. The copycat plant may look like another flower, smell like another flower, feel like another plant, or resemble a male or female pollinator.

GOING BUGGY

Pouyannian mimicry is common among orchids and is named for Maurice-Alexandre Pouyanne, a nineteenth-century French botanist who first observed the phenomenon. In this type of mimicry, the flower of an orchid mimics the look of a female insect, such as a spider or a bee. Male insects of the same insect species are attracted to the flower and try to copulate with it. During this pseudocopulation,

Some orchids have evolved to look like the pollinators they want to attract. For instance, to a male bee, the laughing bumblebee orchid resembles a female bee and smells like a bee too. Looking for mates, many kinds of bees land on the flower.

the males aren't actually having sex with a female insect. They do, however, end up covered in pollen as they try to mate with the orchid flower. When they fly off to other flowers to try to copulate with them as well, the pollen is transferred to the new plant and fertilizes it. Mimicry can extend beyond the visual to tactile (touch) and olfactory (smell) similarities to female insects. For example, some orchid flowers produce the same scents that insects use to attract one another for mating. The scents make the orchids extra alluring to male insects looking for mates.

One orchid that engages in this elaborate form of mimicry is the laughing bumblebee orchid (*Ophrys bombyliflora*), native to lands around the Mediterranean Sea. Not only does it look like a female bumblebee, its scientific name comes from the Greek word for bumblebee (*bombylios*). This plant attracts different species of bees, such as the solitary long-horned bee (*Eucera longicornis*), through the plant's beelike appearance and odor. Yet the one bee that fails to make a beeline to its namesake is the bumblebee! The flower of another

To protect themselves from predators, yellow archangels have evolved to look like stinging nettles. The disguise fools animals that might want to eat their leaves.

orchid, the Australian tongue orchid (*Cryptostylis*), looks so much like a female wasp that male ichneumon wasps, also known as orchid dupe wasps, try to have sex with the flower. When finished with their amorous activity, the males fly away carrying the plant's pollen.

PLAYING DEFENSE

Orchids haven't cornered the market on ninja-like disguises. Some plants engage in Batesian mimicry. It is named for Henry Walter Bates, a nineteenth-century English naturalist who led many expeditions to the Amazon rain forest. In this form of fakery, a harmless life-form mimics the features of a dangerous or repellent plant or animal as a defense mechanism. Botanists suspect this form of mimicry is at work with the yellow archangel (*Lamium galeobdolon*), a type of nettle common in Europe. It has evolved to look like another plant—the dreaded stinging nettle. While yellow archangels are harmless, their leaves resemble those of stinging nettles in shape and color, so browsing animals are fooled and scared off.

One of the most mysterious plant mimics is the genus *Boquila trifoliolata* vine, found in the rain forests of Chile and Argentina in South America. Like most vines, it crawls across the ground, looking for a host plant or tree to wrap itself around. Once it finds a host and starts to grow on it, its normally stumpy and rounded leaves change shape to mimic those of the host plant. For example, the leaves become longer and narrower if that's the shape of the surrounding host plant's leaves. The leaves' color, size, and vein pattern can also change. In fact, the vine can mimic as many as eight different plants.

Some botanists think this mimicry might be a defensive strategy. Maybe the vine hides and protects itself from caterpillars, weevils, and other leaf-eating insects by blending in with the host plant. Another theory is that the vine adopts the appearance of leaves that are toxic to leaf eaters, a form of Batesian mimicry.

If it weren't for the flower blooming from its center, you might mistake this plant—a member of the genus *Lithops*—for a couple of stones. Plants of this genus have evolved to resemble stones so that predators won't eat them.

The vine doesn't even have to touch the plant that it mimics. It only has to be nearby. It's as if the plant can "see" its neighbor. Does it detect the host plant visually or by smell? Does horizontal gene transfer—where genes are passed between two kinds of plants without sexual reproduction—allow for this communication? Scientists don't know.

THE STONE AGE

Some plants not only trick predators, but they trick humans too. While going on a nature walk, you might pick up an interesting-looking stone only to find that it's not a stone at all. Some plants are camouflaged to look like the rocks in their environment. They do this for protection—to trick insects and animals that might want to eat them. Talk about a rocky road to survival!

Plants of the genus *Lithops*, in the deserts of southern Africa, have evolved this defensive behavior. They look like stones so that bush crickets and ground squirrels won't devour them. The name *Lithops* comes from the Greek word *lithos*, meaning "stone," and the plants are also called stone plants, pebble plants, and living stones. Plants of this genus have two thick leaves that are broad and flat on top. The bulk of the plant lives beneath the sand. Only the flat leaf tops are visible, and these are usually dull gray or tan, like the rocks they mimic. Animals looking for a yummy treat trot on by them.

JUST A COINCIDENCE: LOOK-ALIKE FUNGI

Fungi are organisms that obtain food by absorbing it from other living things or by absorbing it from dead, decaying organisms. The part of a fungus involved in reproduction is the fruiting body. This structure produces spores (cells), which grow into new organisms. Some fungi produce spores sexually, some produce spores asexually, and many do both. Some fungi have a symbiotic relationship with certain insects. This helps the fungi with pollination.

The nest-like structures in this photo are actually fruiting bodies on a type of bird's nest fungus called *Cyathus olla*. The "eggs" are spores that will splash out in the rain and grow into new fungi.

    Common fungi include mushrooms and yeast. Some less common fungi display coincidental, often humorous, resemblances to everyday things. For example, young bleeding tooth fungi (*Hydnellum peckii*), found in North America and Europe, look like hunks of chewed bubble gum covered in oozing blood. When they grow older, they look like ordinary brown mushrooms.

    When the bird's nest fungus (*Nidula emodensis*) is ready to reproduce, it grows a fruiting body that resembles a tiny nest filled with eggs. The "eggs" are actually spores that will grow to become new organisms. When rainwater falls into the "nests," which typically grow on decaying wood or feces, the egg-like spores splash out and onto the ground. New bird's nest fungi will grow where the spores land, as long as the soil is nutrient rich.

CRYING FRUIT

The jabuticaba tree (*Plinia cauliflora*) of South America has a unique feature. The fruit of most fruit trees grows and hangs from stems attached to branches. But the round fruit of this tree grows directly on the bark of the tree's trunk and branches (*right*). This makes the tree look as if it is crying big, oily black tears.

The fruit grows all over the tree, even near ground level, so it's easy for animals to reach it. Even animals that don't climb, such as the Brazilian giant tortoise, can feast on the fruit. In fact, the tree gets its name from the tortoises that eat there. In the language of the Tupi people of Brazil, *jabuti* means "tortoise." *Caba* means "place," so the name of the tree means "tortoise place." As animals eat the fruit, many of the seeds in the fruit fall to the ground, where some will take root. The more animals eating the fruit, the more chances the tree has of reproducing and surviving. The small fruit tastes a bit like grapes, and people in South America use it to make jam and juice.

The devil's fingers (*Clathrus archeri*), a mushroom native to Australia, New Zealand, and Tasmania, is one of the strangest and creepiest-looking fungi on Earth. Imagine a cold, dead hand reaching out of the ground—that's exactly what this fungus looks like when its white tentacles burst from the soil and begin to grow. It develops a putrid smell as it matures. That, together with its appearance, is sure to make human passersby scream and run. But carrion flies and other insect pollinators are attracted to the smell.

Bleeding heart flowers attract pollinators that like the color red.

JUST A COINCIDENCE: LOOK-ALIKE PLANTS

Like fungi, some plants resemble other living things. For example, the seedpod of the snapdragon (*Antirrhinum*) looks just like a human skull. Scary! The white berries with black dots on the doll's eyes plant (*Actaea pachypoda*), a poisonous plant native to eastern North America, resemble spooky eyes on stalks. The flowers of the cotton grass plant (*Eriophorum*), commonly found in Iceland, resemble balls of cotton. The cow's udder plant (*Solanum mammosum*) of South America is a relative of the tomato and potato. It resembles a cow's mammary (milk-producing) glands. For these look-alike plants and fungi, the resemblances to other things in nature are just coincidences. The features haven't evolved to visually entice pollinators or to fool predators.

Like the bleeding tooth fungi, many plants look bloody.

MIMICS

The plant world is full of mimics. In Pouyannian mimicry, a flower mimics a female insect to attract the right male pollinator. Batesian mimicry occurs when a harmless species imitates the dangerous characteristics of a harmful species to ward off predators. Botanists have identified many other forms of plant mimicry.

Bakerian mimicry, named after twentieth-century British naturalist Herbert G. Baker, occurs among some genuses of papayas (*Carica*), orchids (*Catasetum*), and begonias. In plants that practice Bakerian mimicry, the female flowers visually mimic the male flowers to trick pollinators into thinking they will find a reward (pollen) on a female flower when one doesn't exist. This trickery ensures that a pollinator will visit the female flower and (assuming that the pollinator has previously visited a male flower) bring pollen to it.

Dodsonian mimicry, named after twentieth-century US botanist Calaway H. Dodson, occurs when the flowers of one species mimic the flowers of another species to lure specific pollinators. Vavilovian mimicry, named after twentieth-century Russian plant geneticist Nikolai Vavilov, is also known as crop mimicry, or weed mimicry. In this form of mimicry, a weed mimics one or more of the characteristics of a plant that is valued by humans, such as wheat or corn. If a weed looks like the food plants growing nearby, farmers are less likely to pull it out and destroy it when weeding their fields. Resembling a valued food plant is a survival mechanism for the weed.

To get the pollen they need for fertilization, some female papaya flowers (*left*) mimic male papaya flowers (*right*). The goal is to trick pollinators into thinking they'll find pollen on the female flower.

Bleeding hearts (*Lamprocapnos spectabilis*) are native to Siberia, northern China, Korea, and Japan and are common in other temperate regions as early-blooming spring garden plants. They have heart-shaped flowers that appear to be dripping blood. Red is a powerful attraction to pollinators, so the bloody-looking flowers help the plant reproduce by attracting the insects needed for fertilization. Perhaps the "bloodiest" of all plants is the dragon blood tree (*Dracaena draco*). It grows in western Morocco and nearby islands in the Atlantic Ocean. When cut or injured, the bark and leaves of this tree ooze sap that looks like blood from a ruptured vein. Sap is important for trees because it transports water and nutrients throughout tree trunks and branches. The dragon blood tree has sap that is toxic to some animals that might try to eat it. However, this thick red sap can be beneficial to humans. When applied to wounds, it stops bleeding and quickens healing. When taken internally, it can relieve digestive problems. Indigenous peoples where the tree grows once used the sap as medicine, and it is also used to make commercial varnishes.

The monkey face orchid (*Dracula simia*) resembles more than one other living thing. The flower of the orchid resembles the smiling face of a small monkey. In fact, the species name *simia* means "monkey" in Latin. And the genus name *Dracula* refers to the orchid's long sepals (parts of the flower below the petals). They resemble Dracula's fangs. This hard-to-believe plant grows at high elevations in the mountains of Ecuador, Colombia, and Peru in South America. The orchid's flower smells like an orange. This odor, as well as the flower's pink-and-white colors, attracts pollinators.

5

GOING TO EXTREMES

NINJAS WERE FAMOUS FOR GOING TO
EXTREME LENGTHS TO DEFEAT THEIR ENEMIES.

They used extreme measures in the activities of spying, assassination,
and guerilla warfare. They lived their lives outside the norm.
Many plants also live outside the norm, in extreme environmental
conditions. These plants have evolved to survive in extra-cold, hot,
and dry climates. Some have evolved to grow in peculiar kinds of soil.
Often extreme and unusual surroundings affect how the plants look
and behave.

SHAPE-SHIFTERS

Arctic willows (*Salix arctica*) grow in the bitterly cold and windy
Arctic regions of the planet. Instead of growing vertically, these plants
grow horizontally. They almost look as if they have been trampled.
Horizontal growth serves a critical purpose in protecting the tiny
shrubs from ferocious Arctic winds. Many mountain plants grow

By growing less than 1 inch (2.5 cm) above the ground, arctic willows protect themselves from the ferocious winds that blow through their northern habitat. The plant's red pollen attracts pollinators in spring.

horizontally for the same reason. By growing low to the ground, they aren't likely to be blown over or blown away by the powerful winds common at high elevations.

Other plants have developed unusual shapes in response to local conditions. For example, sitting on a dormant volcano in Panama in Central America is the Valley of Square Trees. The name says it all. The cottonwood trees there have square trunks, and the growth rings in the interior of the trees grow in squares instead of in the typical circles seen in other trees. University of Florida researchers tried to grow these cottonwood trees in other locations. When they transplanted a few seedlings to another place, the seedlings grew into trees with round trunks. The experiment showed that local conditions in the Valley of Square Trees are responsible for the shape of the trunks.

Baobab trees can store thousands of gallons of water in their trunks. This capacity can be a lifesaver in the drought-prone regions where the trees live.

Baobab trees (*Adansonia*) also have shapes adapted to environmental conditions. These trees, native to Madagascar, Australia, and Africa, can grow to be more than 100 feet (30 m) tall. The tree trunks are exceptionally wide, measuring about 30 feet (9 m) across. They look out of proportion because they are so wide in comparison to the trees' height. Baobab trees are leafless for the majority of the year, giving their naked limbs a rootlike appearance. In fact, some people refer to baobabs as upside-down trees because it looks as if their roots are growing up into the sky instead of down into the earth. A baobab tree's thick trunk can hold a huge amount of water—about 26,000 gallons (98,000 liters). Because the trees live where severe drought is common, water storage is critical to the trees' survival. As they grow, baobab trees become hollow inside. Some people have even created homes inside the hollow trunks. One trunk in South Africa was transformed into a pub (bar), and many baobab trees in the remote Australian outback have been used as temporary prisons.

NATURE OR NURTURE?

The Gryfino forest in Poland, nicknamed the Crooked Forest, is home to about four hundred unusually shaped trees. These pine trees don't grow straight and tall like others of their species or like surrounding trees in the forest. Instead, they all have a nearly identical 90-degree bend at the base of their trunks. Above the bend, the trees curve upward and grow straight toward the sun.

The cause of this unusual shape is a mystery, with theories ranging from Earth's gravitational pull to the effects of heavy snow. Some people believe that human intervention made the trees crooked. They were planted in the 1930s, not long before Germany invaded Poland during World War II (1939–1945). Some theorize that German tanks flattened the saplings (young trees) as they drove through the forest. Another idea is that Polish tree farmers deliberately bent the saplings or otherwise stunted their growth to create the curved trunks, which could be harvested to obtain curved timbers. Shipbuilders might have wanted the curved timbers to strengthen the hulls of ships. Furniture makers might also have valued the timbers for their unusual curves.

Why are these trees in Poland oddly curved at the bottoms? Did people bend them when they were saplings, or did something in the environment create the curves? Botanists do not know for sure.

THE MYSTERIOUS TREE OF LIFE

We all know that plants need water, sunlight, and carbon dioxide to survive. If any one of these isn't available, the plant will die, right? Well, maybe not. One phenomenal plant has survived for more than four hundred years without a permanent source of liquid water. Seriously, no agua! Nicknamed the Tree of Life, it is in the Middle Eastern nation of Bahrain in the middle of a desert. There is no water source anywhere nearby. Thousands of tourists trek through the blinding heat each year to see this miracle.

It is a mesquite tree. These trees are also common in very dry areas of the southwestern United States and Mexico. How do they survive? The answer is that water vapor in the air, as fog, condenses (cools and turns into liquid water) on the trees' leaves. Mesquites also have incredibly long taproots that can locate water deep underground. Scientists suspect that these adaptations hold the Tree of Life's secret to survival.

How has this tree survived for more than four hundred years in the middle of a desert with no lake or river nearby? Nicknamed the Tree of Life, it gathers water vapor from the air and liquid water from deep underground.

The welwitschia (*Welwitschia mirabilis*) has been dubbed the world's most resistant plant for the way it survives severe droughts. It grows only in the Namib Desert of southwestern Africa, and it can live more than two thousand years. This plant grows only two leaves from a single stem. They grow outward like wide green ribbons. Over time, as the leaves wear out, they tear, split, curl, and twist. Dew (water vapor from the air that has condensed, or turned from gas into liquid) settling on the long leaves provides the plant with some of its moisture. A deep taproot also collects water and nutrients from the soil underground. Many smaller roots grow outward from the taproot in all directions. They too collect water and nutrients from the soil.

PLAYING POSSUM

The opossum, a small nocturnal mammal that lives in North America, is famous for playing dead. It doesn't do this on purpose. When confronted by attackers, opossums faint out of fear. The fright sends the animals into a coma-like state that can last from forty minutes to four hours. During this time, an opossum drools, its body goes limp, and it emits a slight smell of decay. Although the animal doesn't do this to deliberately trick predators, the behavior has the effect of sending predators on their way.

Some plants in regions that experience extremes of weather and sunlight can also appear to be playing dead. As with the opossum, this behavior aids in survival. The plants wither to conserve water. They can remain withered for as little as a portion of a day or for up to a year or more. The resurrection fern (*Selaginella lepidophylla*), technically not a fern despite its

The resurrection fern in the top part of this photo looks dead. But it will green up again after a rainstorm (*bottom*).

name, is one of these deceptive plants. Common in the deserts of North and South America, it is healthy in times of plentiful rainfall. But when the weather is extremely hot and dry, the plant dries and shrivels up, taking on the appearance of lifelessness. In this dormant stage, the plant can survive on as little as 3 percent of its daily water needs. (Most other plants will die if they get less than 90 percent of the water they need.) And when the plant is curled up, less of its surface is exposed to strong sunlight, which can evaporate what little water the plant has absorbed in its leaves. An added benefit is that predators, believing the plant is dead, have no interest in eating it. The resurrection fern can lie dormant for years until rain returns. And when the rain comes . . . boom! The plant bursts into a green mass of life as if resurrected from the dead.

Lichens, which are dual organisms consisting of fungi and algae growing together, can survive in some of the most extreme conditions on Earth. They can live 18,000 feet (5,500 m) high in the Himalayan mountains and close to the South Pole in Antarctica. Few other plants and animals can survive in such cold environments. In the long winter season, when water is trapped in ice and snow, lichens survive by going dormant. They shrivel up like a deceased plant but remain alive. In the short spring season, when some of the ice and snow melt and moisture again becomes available, lichens suck it up at extraordinary speed and in great quantities. In ten minutes, lichens can absorb half their body weight in water, seemingly bursting back to life. The effect is like putting a dried-up sponge into a tub of water. Puff!

Many people keep cacti as houseplants because they are easy to keep alive. They require little water and attention—the perfect plant for those who do not have a green thumb. Cacti have evolved to survive in the extreme environments found in deserts. And they have many tricks up their prickly sleeves. They can store water during dry spells. And like the resurrection fern, they can go dormant and shrivel up during droughts, looking dead or nearly dead. When rain falls, they rapidly suck up the moisture and burst back to life, much like lichens do. The dormancy stage is key to their survival, as it allows them to conserve vital energy until water becomes available.

A cactus, such as this *Eriosyce rodentiophila* in the Atacama Desert of Chile in South America, can live for almost a year without a direct source of water. It gets by largely on water vapor that condenses when temperatures drop in the desert at night.

Another death pretender is the eriosyce (*Eriosyce odieri*), native to Chile in South America. This type of cactus can fake its death like the heroine Juliet does in William Shakespeare's *Romeo and Juliet*, a tragic play about two star-crossed lovers. The plant can lie low, literally, and remain dormant for years awaiting rain. When it finally gets enough water, it revives and produces a beautiful yellow, pink, or orange flower, depending on the species.

6

GET A MOVE ON

PLANTS CAN GENERALLY BE CHARACTERIZED
BY ONE WORD: *SESSILE*—THEY ARE UNMOVING.
PLANTS CAN'T RUN AND CATCH THE FOOD
THEY NEED LIKE ANIMALS CAN.

Plants can't fly to a more hospitable place or move out of town to gain additional sunlight on overcast days. And plants can't travel freely if they face danger from other plants and animals. Or can they?

Some plants actually do move, and they do so as quietly as ninjas. They do it for one vital reason: survival. They move in many different ways. Some plants gain mobility by attaching their stems and seeds to people and animals to get free rides to new places to grow. Some kinds of leaves move toward the sun at certain times of the day to obtain maximum amounts of sunlight. Other leaves fold inward when something touches them, as a defense against predators. Many flowers close in the rain to keep their pollen from getting wet.

Cholla cacti, such as these in Joshua Tree National Park in California, use their spines in two ways. First, the spines keep predators from eating the cacti. Second, the spines stick to human and animal passersby, which then carry segments of cactus stems to new places. The stems will root in the soil there and grow into new cactus plants.

GRAB AND GO

The spines of the jumping cholla cactus (*Cylindropuntia fulgida*) and the teddy bear cholla cactus (*Cylindropuntia bigelovii*) will hitch a ride with anyone or anything that passes by or even lightly touches them. On a walk through the deserts of the southwestern United States, you might think these plants—which grow as tall as 8 feet (2.4 m)—are reaching out and grabbing you. You might end up with pieces of spiny cactus stem stuck to your skin or clothing. Talk about nature's hitchhikers! But don't try to pull out the spines with your hands, because they will stick to your hands too. It's best to quickly brush them away using a comb or a stick.

Cacti mainly use their spines as a defense against predators. But the spines also aid in reproduction. Chollas and some other cacti can reproduce asexually. When their spiny stem segments fall to the ground or an animal or human carries them to a new place, they take root in the soil and grow into identical copies of the parent plant. This is called clonal propagation.

The seedpods of the unicorn plant (*Proboscidea*) hitch rides to new areas too. Native to the southwestern United States and northern Mexico, this plant is also called the devil's claw, or the devil's horn, because of the long, curved hooks on its seedpods.

STUCK ON YOU

One day in the 1940s, a Swiss engineer named George de Mestral took his dog for a hike in the forest. The dog rubbed against burdock burrs, which stuck to its fur. At home, after picking the burrs off his dog, de Mestral studied them. The burrs gave him the idea for a fastening system consisting of two pieces of fabric. One was covered with tiny nylon hooks like those on the burdock burrs. The other was covered with small nylon loops. When the two pieces were pressed together, they stayed stuck until someone pulled them apart. De Mestral named his invention Velcro.

In the twenty-first century, Velcro is used to hang pictures, fasten shoes and clothing, and organize household items. Astronauts living and working on the International Space Station even use Velcro to attach tools and equipment to the walls inside their spacecraft. Without Velcro, the gear would float around inside the station. It wouldn't just sit on tabletops or the floor as it would on Earth, because out in space, gravity doesn't pull objects to the ground.

Burdock burrs, which stick to animal hair and fur, inspired the invention of Velcro.

These sharp claws can easily stick to boots, shoes, or animal hooves. When the people or animals walk, their weight crushes the seedpods and disperses the seeds. Even though the pink-and-yellow flowers of the unicorn plant are pretty, you'll want to stay far away from it. Like the famous metal hand claw weapon of the ninja, the plant's claws can rip your skin!

SLIDE ON OVER

The galloping moss (*Grimmia ovalis*) doesn't really gallop, but it does move (though slowly). Mosses are small nonflowering plants that grow in shady, moist areas. They form dense mats on trees, rocks, and soil—as long as the spot is cool, moist, and dark. The galloping moss is native to Arctic regions, high altitudes, and other places where permafrost (layers of subsoil that are permanently frozen throughout the year) is common. The moss attaches itself to lichens on rocky slopes and then moves slowly downhill with the lichens. The lichens and the moss move together, leaving a visible trail on the bare rock, showing where they have been.

Botanists believe that the plant movement is related to water in cracks in the rocks beneath the mosses and the lichens. At night the water freezes into ice and expands, putting pressure on the cracks and making them break open a little more. When the ice melts in the daytime, the water seeps deeper into the cracks. When the water refreezes at night, the cracks grow even larger, eventually causing the rock to break apart. Botanists think that as the rocks crack and move, the mosses and lichens move too. This plant movement from the freezing and thawing of rocks or soil is known as solifluction floating.

VINE AND DANDY

Strangler figs and other parasitic vines move to find host plants to feed on. One remarkable example is the dodder (*Cuscuta*), a vine found in temperate and tropical regions.

The dodder is a clever parasite that "sniffs out" chemicals emitted by potential hosts. Once it has attached itself to a host, the dodder sucks out the nutrients it needs, often killing the host in the process.

The dodder begins its life like many other plants. It grows from seeds and puts roots into the soil. But once it sprouts, it starts looking for a host plant. When it finds one, it wraps itself around the plant's stem. Then it inserts appendages called haustoria into the host's vascular system, the tissues that carry water and nutrients throughout the plant. The dodder sucks out sugars and other photosynthates produced during photosynthesis. Once the dodder begins feeding on its host, its original roots wither and die in the soil, since the dodder is no longer extracting its own nutrients from the soil.

A single dodder can attach itself to multiple hosts. How does it find them? Recent scientific research suggests that the dodder "sniffs out" chemicals emitted into the air by nearby hosts. The dodder is attracted to those chemicals, growing toward new host plants like a ninja stealthily sneaking up on its next victim. When the dodder steals water and nutrients from its host, it often kills the host. In the United States and elsewhere, dodders frequently kill crops such as alfalfa, flax, and potatoes. Many countries have laws prohibiting the import of dodder seeds. Farmers try to combat the plants' spread with herbicides that kill them and by planting nonhost crops such as grasses for several years after a dodder infestation.

TOUCH-ME-NOT

While some plants move by attaching themselves to other organisms or move to feed on host plants, other plants move without changing locations. Their more subtle bends, wiggles, and twists are no less critical to their survival, however. These movements are used for defense or to ensure adequate opportunities for photosynthesis.

The sensitive plant (*Mimosa pudica*), native to South America and Central America, is a mobile plant that lives up to its touchy name. This plant's leaves are hypersensitive. They fold inward and droop when something touches, shakes, or otherwise disturbs the plant—a form of thigmonasty.

The leaves of the sensitive plant fold up and droop when they are touched. The folded leaves (*center*) are less appealing to predators, which might think the plant is dead and leave it alone.

MEXICAN JUMPING BEANS

A favorite at gift shops in the US Southwest, the Mexican jumping bean is actually the seed capsule of a Mexican shrub (*Sebastiana pavoniana*). Female moths of the species *Laspeyresia saltitans* lay their eggs on the plant's flowers in early summer. The eggs grow into wormlike larvae.

Looking for food, a larva will chomp its way into a seed capsule inside the flower and close the hole with the silk it makes as it grows. When the larva inside gets warm, such as when the seed capsule is held in a person's hand, it begins to twitch. This movement makes it seem as if the capsule is jumping in response to human touch.

This is likely a defensive move, since closed, droopy leaves look less attractive to herbivorous bugs and animals than open and upright ones. The plant's leaves reopen several minutes after the danger has passed.

The species name *pudica* is derived from the Latin word for "shy." This name makes sense when you consider how the leaves fold up and seem to hide when they're touched. The Hebrew name for *Mimosa pudica*, when translated into English, is "the don't-touch-me plant."

HERE COMES THE SUN

Sunlight, not touch, causes immature sunflower buds (*Helianthus*) to move. As they are growing, the buds face toward the sun, following its westward movement during the day. In this way, sunflower buds maximize the amount of direct sunlight they capture. As a sunflower matures, however, its stem stiffens and it no longer moves to face the sun.

The sunflower is not alone in moving toward the sun. In fact, moving toward the sunlight is not at all unusual for plants, although most don't move in a dramatic way. Chemical receptors in the tips of plant shoots sense sunlight and send that information to other parts of the plant. Then the plant moves to face the light. British naturalist Charles Darwin wrote about this behavior in his 1880 book *The Power*

Young sunflowers exhibit heliotropism. They move to face the sun as it travels across the sky in the course of a day.

*of Movement in Plant*s. He noted, "There are extremely few [plants], of which some part . . . does not bend toward lateral light." This sunlight-seeking behavior is known as solar tracking, or heliotropism.

The word *heliotropism* is derived from the Greek words *helios,* meaning "sun" and *tropos,* meaning "turn." This behavior is different from but related to photoperiodism. With photoperiodism, plants measure the amount of light they take in and then flower in response to the light.

7

CATCHING FIRE

ANCIENT NINJAS OFTEN USED ARSON. THEY
SET FIRE TO ENEMY CAMPS AND CASTLES
USING EXPLOSIVES, FIRE ARROWS, TORCHES,
AND OTHER DEVICES.

Fire is a powerful force of nature. One of the greatest fears for anyone living near a wooded area is a forest fire. Each summer, especially in dry regions, the news is filled with stories of fire racing across great tracts of land, consuming everything in its path, from trees to homes.

For trees and other plants, however, forest fires are not always a disaster. Some plants have developed unique ways to survive fires. In fact, many pine trees and other plants that live in areas where fire is common actually rely on fires to open up the tough capsules that contain their seeds. An example is the manzanita (*Arctostaphylos*), a common evergreen shrub in California. Its seeds don't germinate without the high heat from a fire.

Fire helps plants in other ways. When a fire blazes through a forest, it burns up dried or decayed organic (living or once living) matter, such as

Eucalyptus trees contain highly flammable oil, so they explode into flames during forest fires. Layers of dead leaves and bark surrounding the trees intensify the flames.

dead trees and plants on the forest floor. Like all organic matter, the dead plants still contain nutrients such as nitrogen and phosphorus. Fire quickly releases the nutrients, returning them to the soil much more rapidly than does the slow natural process of decomposition. Some plants are quick to take advantage of the added nutrients after a fire. Examples are aspen trees, snapdragons, wild cucumbers, and blueberry bushes, which burst back to life relatively quickly on burned tracks of land. In this way, they get a jump on the competition. They flourish in the fire-fertilized soil, reestablishing themselves before other species are able to grow back.

BURN, BABY, BURN

The paperbark tree (*Melaleuca*) is naturally fire resistant. This tree, native to Australia, New Zealand, and New Caledonia, has white, spongy bark that easily flakes off or can be ripped away. Over the centuries, indigenous peoples have used the bark to make canoes, roofs for houses, and shields for battle. The tree reproduces through its seeds, which usually fall onto the soil close to the parent tree.

RULES AND REGULATIONS

When Americans return from travel outside the United States, government agents at US airports ask them to report any plants or seeds they have brought back with them from abroad. Mostly travelers are not allowed to bring plants or seeds into the United States. Why? Foreign insects could be hiding among the leaves of these plants. These bugs might end up preying on US food crops, which have not evolved any defenses to protect themselves from the unfamiliar bugs. In addition, some foreign plants, such as Australia's paperbark tree, are considered invasive species in the United States. Invasive species (both plants and animals) are newcomers that spread rapidly in their new environments, with no natural predators to keep their numbers in check. (The snout beetle keeps the paperbark tree in check in Australia.) Without predators, invasive species can quickly come to dominate an ecosystem. They might consume all the natural resources, such as water and minerals from the soil, sometimes driving native plants to extinction.

Many US government agencies, such as the US Department of Agriculture (USDA) and the Environmental Protection Agency (EPA), work tirelessly to keep foreign plants from entering the United States. US laws such as the Plant Protection Act and the Alien Species Prevention and Enforcement Act limit the introduction of invasive species into the United States and monitor the distribution of seeds and plants from foreign countries. If invasive plants do establish themselves in the United States, the US Forest Service, the USDA, and other agencies work with homeowners, landowners, and farmers to eliminate or control the invaders.

The species not only survives fire but actually thrives because of fire. Why? When a forest fire rips through paperbark tree habitat, the trees' flaky outer layers burn away, but the moist inner layers do not burn. The heat of the fire also opens the trees' dried seedpods. They release their seeds. Then they lodge in nearby soil and grow into new paperbark trees. The tree can produce up to twenty million seeds per year.

The jack pine (*Pinus banksiana*), native to the central United States and Canada, also relies on forest fires for seed dispersal. The tree's cones are glued shut with a sticky, hard resin. Only intense heat, like that from a forest fire, will melt the resin and allow the cones to burst open and release their seeds. Botanists describe such cones as serotinous—they release their seeds only in response to an environmental trigger, such as a fire. Seeds will remain in jack pine cones for years until a trigger opens the cones.

Giant sequoia trees (*Sequoiadendron giganteum*), also called Sierra redwoods, are native to the Sierra Nevada range of California. They are some of the largest trees in the world. They can grow up to 300 feet (91 m) tall and up to 30 feet (9 m) across. The tree's serotinous cones contain about two hundred seeds each. Like jack pinecones, giant sequoia cones rely on fire to burst them open so their seeds will disperse.

Some plants depend on smoke rather than fire. An example is the desert raisin (*Solanum centrale*), a small Australian bush that produces fruit resembling raisins when it dries. The seeds of this plant lie dormant in the soil until smoke from burning plants signals for them to germinate and sprout. Some plant biologists think that

The seedpods of paperbark trees in Australia need fire to open. The trees' dry, papery bark burns during fires, but the inner layers of wood are moist and do not burn.

Only intense heat will open the cones of jack pine trees, allowing them to release their seeds. That's why forest fires are critical to the trees' reproduction.

butenolide, an active ingredient in smoke, triggers this response. The desert raisin and other plants that sprout in response to smoke are found in fire-prone areas. This makes sense because the seeds need smoke to begin growing. Scientists think that smoke might alert the seeds that good growing conditions, such as the nutrient-rich soil created by a fire, are on the way.

PYROMANIA!

Pyro is the Greek word for "fire." A pyromaniac is someone who has an intense compulsion to set fires. While pyromania is a disorder in humans, the need (and ability) to start fires in plants is something quite different. The gas plant, also known as the burning bush (*Dictamnus*), thrives in warm woodlands in Europe, parts of Africa, and in much of Asia. On hot summer nights, this fire-starting plant naturally produces large amounts of flammable oil containing the compound isoprene. According to plant biologists, isoprene normally functions as a cooling agent, protecting the gas plant from heat stress caused by the high temperatures and intense sunlight in regions where it lives. This sticky flammable oil covers the plant and can be ignited by any form of fire, such as a lightning strike. If a person were to strike a match to a gas plant, the whole plant would burst into flames. Even when the plant is not burning, its oil can create raised welts and oozing blisters on any humans and other animals that come into contact with it. This ability is an effective defense mechanism against predators.

Eucalyptus trees (genus *Eucalyptus*) are also pyromaniacs. These trees, native to Australia, grow in tropical and temperate climates and produce fragrant yet flammable oil. When a forest fire passes through an area populated with eucalyptus trees, the oil intensifies the flames. The ground around many eucalyptus trees is covered by a thick layer of dead leaves. During dry weather, eucalyptus bark peels off in long streamers. When fire hits the bark, leaves, and oil, the trees can explode in flames, covering the surrounding area with toxins and emitting a bluish-gray cloud of gas. The tree itself is actually very fire resistant.

After a fire, the tree is still able to reproduce through shoots that sprout from under its bark.

Pampas grass (*Cortaderia*), native to southern parts of South America, grows up to 10 feet (3 m) high. It also intensifies wildfires by sucking up scarce water in drought-prone areas, leaving surrounding plants without enough moisture. These plants then die, creating heaps of light, dry, and highly flammable material around the pampas grass. When wildfires strike, they find plenty to burn, including the pampas grass. As a species, however, pampas is fire resistant. After a fire, although the grass fronds die, the plant's root crown (the top of the root system, from which new stems grow) easily regenerates.

OVER THE RAINBOW

Most tree bark is a shade of brown, although some bark is white. But the rainbow eucalyptus tree (*Eucalyptus deglupta*), on islands of Southeast Asia, doesn't stick with one color. Its inner bark is green. Over time, as the bark matures, the color changes to blue, purple, orange, red, and finally brown. Then the bark falls off the tree, revealing a new layer of green bark underneath. The bark doesn't shed all at once, however. Little pieces of bark break off all over the tree at different times. As a result, this tree is multicolored throughout the year.

This rapid bark exfoliation (shedding) provides several advantages to the rainbow eucalyptus. Since the tree is incredibly fast growing, the quick exfoliation allows its trunk to expand rapidly. The areas of thin shedding bark also allow the tree to lose water quickly during transpiration. Trees that cycle water through their systems quickly can grow more quickly.

The bark of the rainbow eucalyptus tree changes color over time. On each tree, strands of bark show various colors, as layers of bark fall off the tree at different times.

PLANTS AND HUMANS: A LOVE LETTER

NO DISCUSSION ABOUT PLANTS WOULD
BE COMPLETE WITHOUT LOOKING AT THE
RELATIONSHIP BETWEEN PLANTS AND HUMANS.
PLANTS ARE KEY TO LIFE ON EARTH.

People and animals eat them, and they produce the oxygen we breathe. Since prehistoric times, people have used the sap, bark, oils, and leaves of plants to make medicine. For thousands of years, plants have also captured the imagination of writers, artists, and other creative minds worldwide.

American naturalist William Bartram (1739–1823) used both words and illustrations to share his love of plants. He lived in Pennsylvania during the North American colonial period and the early years of the United States. In 1791 he published *The Travels of William Bartram*, detailing his journey through Florida, Georgia, and the Carolinas and his exploration of the region's natural botanical beauty. This book is still prized in the twenty-first century as a landmark of American nature writing.

The popular children's book writer Shel Silverstein honored our leafy friends in his classic 1964 illustrated book *The Giving Tree.* Pop star Stevie Wonder wrote and recorded an entire album in 1979 about plants *Stevie Wonder's Journey through "The Secret Life of Plants."* He created it for a nature documentary of the same name. Plants continue to appear in pop songs, such as "Nothing Compares 2 U," written by Prince and sung by Sinead O'Connor in 1990. English poet Felix Dennis founded a tree-planting charity in 2003 to reforest a part of England near

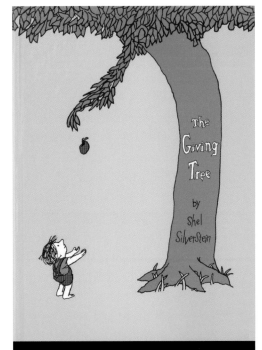

The Giving Tree, a much-loved children's book, explores one boy's lifelong relationship with a tree. Since ancient times, humans have created stories, songs, and artwork to honor the plants around them.

his home. Since then, workers with his charity have planted more than one million trees. Dennis is famous for his poem "Whosoever Plants a Tree." It reminds readers that planting trees is like winking at immortality—that is, sending a signal that the natural world will continue forever.

Plants have also found their way into popular video games, TV shows, and movies. In the video game *Plants vs. Zombies*, a homeowner uses plants to fight off a horde of walking dead attackers. In an episode of *The Simpsons* called "The Mysterious Voyage of Homer," the Simpson dad eats several Guatemalan insanity peppers that cause him to hallucinate a mysterious journey. *Little Shop of Horrors*, a famous 1982 Broadway play turned into a successful 1986 movie, recounts the tale of a carnivorous plant—created by a nerdy florist named Seymour—that develops a taste for human blood. And in the 2015 film *The Martian*, a stranded astronaut played by Matt Damon devotes much of his time to growing plants on the inhospitable planet Mars, where he is stranded.

Plants aren't new to literature and culture. Humans have told tales about plants since ancient times. One of the oldest is the *Epic of Gilgamesh*, composed in ancient Mesopotamia (a region of the Middle East) in about 2100 BCE. In this tale, the hero seeks a magical plant that holds the key to immortality. Travel to Asia and you'll encounter a plethora of ancient stories about bamboo. For example, a creation myth from the Philippines tells how the world's first man was born inside a stalk of a bamboo plant.

Throughout history beans have been an important food source for many peoples, except the ancient Egyptians, who believed beans were too sacred to eat. Many American Indian groups, such as the Iroquois and the Hopi, have honored beans through their festivals and tales. The famous ancient Greek philosopher Pythagoras (570–495 BCE), well-known to geometry students for his Pythagorean theorem, believed the souls of dead people lived inside beans. Think about that the next time you eat a burrito!

WHERE HAS THE LOVE GONE?

While plants serve vital functions in our lives and have fascinated writers, musicians, and casual observers throughout history, our modern use of plants is increasingly out of balance with the natural world. For example, people around the globe—especially in industrialized nations such as the United States—rely on carbon-based fossil fuels (petroleum, natural gas, and coal) to power their vehicles and factories and to heat their homes. Fossil fuels are formed from the remains of ancient plants and animals. Burning these fuels releases huge amounts of carbon dioxide gas into the atmosphere. This gas and other greenhouse gases (such as methane, ozone, and nitrous oxide) trap the sun's heat near Earth. Over time, as humans have released more greenhouse gases into the atmosphere, Earth's temperature has risen.

The village of Eita in the Pacific island nation of Kiribati was largely submerged by flooding in the fall of 2015. Rising sea levels endanger islands like this and the plants and animals that live there. Kiribati may be completely underwater within a few decades.

Rising temperatures have led to melting ice at the North Pole and South Pole, rising sea levels as the polar ice has melted, and changing global weather patterns, including more intense storms and more severe droughts. Increasing droughts and storms have left some human communities devastated and have killed food crops and other plants. Droughts, storms, and rising sea levels have also forced thousands of people—known as climate migrants—to leave their homes and seek new lives in distant regions or distant countries.

Along with climate change, each year Earth loses more than 30 million acres (12 million hectares) of forests—mostly rain forests in tropical parts of the world. People cut down or burn the forests to make room for farms, roads, mines, factories, and homes. With fewer trees to take in carbon dioxide, Earth in the twenty-first century has 30 percent more heat-trapping carbon dioxide in its atmosphere than it did 150 years ago. And that's on top of the carbon released from burning fossil fuels. Deforestation not only contributes to climate change, but it also has destroyed the homes and ancient lifeways of indigenous peoples in many tropical regions.

Plants have always been an important source of food for humans. Yet modern consumers rely on only about thirty plants for 90 percent of their food. Many of the most common food crops, such as corn and wheat, are grown on huge tracts of land devoted to just one crop. Known as monoculture, the cultivation of a single crop can harm the environment. For example, corn pulls large amounts of nitrogen from the soil. So on farms that grow only corn, farmers must apply a lot of chemical fertilizer to the soil to replace the lost nitrogen. During rainstorms, excess chemical fertilizer runs off farm fields into local streams and rivers. The polluted water eventually flows to the ocean. On many large, industrialized farms, workers also use chemical pesticides and herbicides to kill bugs and weeds. These chemicals

With their heavy use of chemical pesticides and herbicides, large industrial farms contribute to air and water pollution. Growing corn requires vast amounts of water and also pulls large amounts of nitrogen from the soil. The organic farming movement provides an alternative that is friendlier to Earth.

pollute the air and water and even contaminate the food crops that people eventually eat.

In the United States, many farmers have switched from growing food crops to growing corn that can be converted into fuel for vehicles. Growing corn requires tremendous amounts of precious water, and critics argue that it would be better to use this water to grow crops to feed people than to grow corn to make fuel. Some farmers choose to raise pigs, cattle, and other animals that will be slaughtered for food rather than growing food plants. Per acre, livestock provides far less food than plants. So we could feed more people by planting food crops than we could by raising animals on the same land.

While humans tend to select their food from a very small set of plants, humans use about seventy thousand plant species for medicinal purposes. Many newly created medicines are derived from rain forest plants. For example, a medicine made from the Madagascar periwinkle has saved the lives of more than one hundred thousand children in the United States who suffer from acute lymphocytic leukemia. Only 1 percent of rain forest plants have been studied for their potential use as medicines, leaving a wealth of opportunity for future scientific breakthroughs. But we have to act fast. About 68 percent of all plants on Earth (most in the world's rain forests) are threatened species, in danger of going extinct, as humans continue to destroy their habitats through deforestation.

FINDING SOLUTIONS

Many global citizens are working to fight climate change and to protect plants and food crops. For example, in many urban areas around the world, gardens are springing up on the roofs of office buildings and restaurants. The gardens help shade the buildings in summer and also provide local restaurants with edible plants. Farmers' markets are popular all around the world. They provide consumers with locally raised plant foods—many of them organic, or grown without chemical pesticides and fertilizers.

Organic foods have been moving beyond the farmers' market to the mainstream supermarket. Between 2002 and 2011, US production of organic crops increased almost 250 percent. Annual sales of organic foods topped $81.3 billion in 2012, and sales are expected to grow by about 14 percent each year until at least 2018. Since organic farmers grow fruits and vegetables without harmful chemicals, organic farms don't pose threats to birds, other small animals, and water supplies. And many stores sell organic goods grown locally. This benefits local farmers and reduces the amount of fossil fuels needed to transport food from farms to stores.

In many countries, tree-planting projects are taking off. The Great Green Wall Initiative was the idea of Olusegun Obasanjo, an army general and former president of Nigeria, in 2005. This project to plant trees at the southern edge of the Sahara in Africa is aimed at preventing desertification (the spreading of deserts onto formerly fertile land). The effort has led to improved soil fertility and increased crop yields in many African countries. Kenyan environmental activist Wangari Maathai founded the Green Belt Movement in 1977 when she learned that rural Kenyan women had to walk ever-greater distances to get firewood because local rivers were drying up, so fewer trees

One way humans can fight deforestation and climate change is by planting trees. Members of the Green Belt Movement, started in the late 1970s by Kenyan environmental activist Wangari Maathai (1940–2011), *above*, have planted more than fifty-one million trees in Kenya. In 2004 Maathai became the first African woman to receive the Nobel Peace Prize.

were growing on riverbanks. Women participating in the Green Belt Movement have planted more than fifty-one million trees in Kenya.

On a grander scale, some nations are looking at ways to reduce carbon emissions. In 2015 the United Nations convened a meeting in Paris, France, where representatives of countries from around the world talked about fighting climate change. These Paris Climate Talks resulted in 195 countries agreeing to explore efforts to reduce deforestation and reduce carbon emissions. Additional efforts to fight deforestation include the Billion Tree Campaign. Launched in 2006 by the United Nations Environment Programme and the Amazon Fund of Brazil, the project raises money to prevent, monitor, and combat the rapid destruction of rain forests.

TEENS MAKE A DIFFERENCE

What can you do to help plants? Start in your own neighborhood. Ask an adult and some friends to help you plant a small garden in your yard or at a nearby community plot. Work with teachers and classmates to start a garden at your school or in your neighborhood. Walk or bike to school instead of driving there. Or take a bus, train, or subway. Mass transportation is much better for the environment than driving because dozens of people traveling in one vehicle use less fuel and create less pollution than dozens of people each traveling in an individual car. Send e-mails to your local government officials, asking

With her HAPPY Organization, Haile Thomas, of Tucson, Arizona, teaches other kids about cooking, gardening, and healthy eating.

for their help in providing more green space in your community and for protecting endangered plants. Ask them to join the fight against climate change.

Many teens are working to protect the globe. For instance, in Massachusetts, Olivia Gieger and Shamus Miller of Wellesley High School and Isabel Kain and James Coakley of Boston Latin School sued their state in 2011 for failing to reduce greenhouse gas emissions. And in 2016, they won! Some teens are leading efforts to switch from fossil fuels to nonpolluting energy sources such as solar and wind power. Other kids are encouraging their peers to power down appliances when they're not in use, to limit water use, and to spread the word about ways to fight climate change. In small ways, each of us can make a difference.

It's time to renew our love for trees and plants of all varieties. Even with the ninja-like qualities many plants possess—their stealth, fierce competitive nature, and sometimes deadly tactics to ward off predators—they cannot overcome the destructive effects of human behavior. We need plants for our own survival and for the health of our planet. In return, plants need our help. Through education, increased awareness, and targeted efforts to combat climate change and to save plant life around the globe, we can continue to benefit from and enjoy the secret and remarkable world of plants.

GLOSSARY

abiotic: nonliving chemical and physical parts of an environment, such as sunlight, temperature, wind patterns, and precipitation (snow and rain), that affect how a plant grows

active trap: a type of trap, including closing (snap) traps and trapdoors (suction traps), common to some species of carnivorous plants. These traps use rapid plant movement to catch their prey.

asexual reproduction: a type of reproduction, common in some plants, in which new organisms are formed from the cells of a parent organism, inheriting the genes of the single parent only

Bakerian mimicry: a type of imitation in the plant world in which a female flower mimics the male flower within the same species of plants. This form of mimicry ensures pollination.

Batesian mimicry: a type of imitation in the plant world in which a harmless species of plant looks like a toxic species. This mimicry is a form of defense to repel predators.

binomial nomenclature: a scientific naming system for plants and animals consisting of only two words—the genus (biological ranking) and the species (specific kind of plant or animal within that ranking)

botany: the scientific study of plant structures, behavior, and characteristics. Scientists who study botany are called botanists.

cambium: a layer of tissue between a plant's bark and its inner wood. Cell growth takes place in the cambium, which also transports water and nutrients throughout the plant.

carnivorous: meat eating or insect eating. Some plants are carnivorous. They trap and digest insects as a source of nutrition.

chlorophyll: a green chemical pigment found in plant leaves. Chlorophyll absorbs energy from sunlight. This light energy combines with carbon dioxide and water to create glucose, a type of sugar that plants turn into food, and other nutrients.

clonal propagation: a form of asexual reproduction in plants in which a plant creates a new plant without fertilization. The new plant is genetically the same as the adult plant.

condense: when water vapor turns into liquid water. When water vapor condenses on plant leaves, they are able to use the water for photosynthesis.

cone: a scaly structure that holds the seeds necessary for the reproduction of certain trees and shrubs. Among conifers (cone-bearing plants), pollen forms inside male cones and ovules form inside female cones. The wind carries pollen from male cones to female cones for fertilization. Sometimes fire will play a role too as it is needed to burst open the tightly sealed seed cones.

deforestation: the rapid cutting down or burning of trees in a forest

deoxyribonucleic acid (DNA): the molecules that carry all the genetic information in an organism

Dodsonian mimicry: a form of mimicry in the plant world in which the flower of one plant species looks like the flower of another species to lure a specific pollinator

dormancy: a period in a plant's life when growth and movement are temporarily stopped. Many plants go dormant during times of environmental stress, such as drought.

ecosystem: a community of living and nonliving things that rely on one another for survival. The members of an ecosystem include the plants, animals, water sources, rock formations, and soil found in a certain place.

egg: in plants, female reproductive cells that develop inside ovules. When eggs are fertilized by sperm (male reproductive cells), ovules grow into seeds.

evaporation: the process by which liquid water turns into water vapor. Water evaporates after it passes out of leaves during transpiration.

evolution: changes in the characteristics or behaviors of plants over many generations. Plants often evolve as they adapt to environmental changes, competition with other plants, threats from predators, and other outside influences.

extinction: the death of the last member of a species. Plant species can go extinct if they cannot obtain the resources they need for photosynthesis, defend themselves against predators, or reproduce.

fertilization: in plants, the chemical change that occurs when sperm enter eggs inside ovules. After fertilization, ovules turn into seeds.

fruiting body: an umbrella-shaped structure on a fungus that produces spores. Spores grow to become new fungi.

fungi: non-plant, living organisms that obtain food by absorbing it from living or dead organisms. Common fungi include mildews, molds, and mushrooms.

genes: chemical structures made of deoxyribonucleic acid that are found in the cells of all living things. Genes determine the characteristics of living organisms. Parents pass on genes to their offspring.

germinate: to begin to grow, typically from a seed

glucose: a sugar made during photosynthesis and a necessary nutrient for plants

grafting: connecting two sections—the rootstock and the scion—of two different plants to form a single new plant. When the two sections are wedged tightly together, their cambiums grow new cells and fuse into a single unit.

heliotropism: the movement of plants in response to sunlight

hormones: in plants, chemical substances that control growth, cell division, fruit ripening, dormancy, and other life cycle behaviors

inflorescence: a group, or cluster, of flowers arranged on a single plant stem

insectivores: plants that eat insects to get nutrients, such as nitrogen and phosphorous, not found in the soil where they grow; also known as carnivores

invasive species: plants and animals that grow quickly in new environments because they have few or no natural predators to keep their populations in check. Invasive species can drive native species to extinction.

larvae: certain insects and other animals in their earliest form, right after hatching. Many insect larvae are wormlike.

lichens: plantlike organisms made up of algae and fungi growing together. Most lichens grow on soil, rocks, or tree bark.

mosses: small, green nonflowering plants. Mosses often form dense mats in moist, shady areas on rocks, trees, and soil.

mucilage: a thick, gluey substance formed by plants and important in retaining water, dispersing seeds, and storing food

mutation: a change in the genetic material of a plant or animal, which may be passed on to its offspring. Some mutations harm organisms, some are beneficial, and some are neither harmful nor helpful. Some mutations happen suddenly and others after exposure to ultraviolet radiation or chemicals.

natural selection: the process by which living things pass on traits that help them survive in their environment. With each successive generation, the favorable traits become more common and the less favorable traits die out.

nectar: a sugar-rich liquid produced by plants in glands called nectaries, often in the plant's flower. Nectar attracts pollinators.

parasite: a plant or animal that feeds off another living thing, called a host. Parasitic plants do not make their own food. They attach themselves to the trunks and branches of other plants to extract nutrients from them.

passive trap: a type of trap, including pitfall traps and flypaper (adhesive) traps, common to some species of carnivorous plants. In these traps, insects get stuck inside a plant's slippery walls or stick to substances produced by the plant.

permafrost: permanently frozen soil that is usually located at high altitudes or in Earth's polar regions

phloem: plant tissue that conducts food from the leaves to other parts of the plant

photoperiodism: the response by plants to changes in sunlight, such as the length of days. This affects when plants bloom.

photosynthesis: the process by which green plants combine sunlight, carbon dioxide, and water to make food

pollen: tiny grains produced in the male organs of plants' flowers and cones. Sperm, or male reproductive cells, develop inside pollen. For plants to reproduce, pollen from male organs must travel to female plant organs.

pollen vectors: living and nonliving things that help to pollinate a plant, such as insects and wind

pollination: the transfer of pollen from the male part of a flower to the female part of a flower or from a male cone to a female cone. Insects, birds, and wind often carry pollen from male to female plant organs.

Pouyannian mimicry: a form of mimicry in the plant world in which a flower evolves to resemble and sometimes smell like a female of a certain insect species to attract males of that species. Male insects come to the flower looking to mate with a female but end up covered in pollen, which they will transfer to other flowers, assisting plants in fertilization.

predator: an animal that lives by feeding on other animals or on plants

prey: an animal hunted for food

pseudocopulation: a behavior in which a male insect attempts to have sex with a plant, mistaking it for a female insect. In doing so, the male insect gets covered in pollen, which aids in fertilizing the plant.

respiration: the process by which plants break down the food they have created and convert it into the energy necessary for growth

ripen: in fruits, to mature to a point where their flesh is soft, tasty, and ready to eat

sap: liquid found in the stems, roots, and leaves of plants. Sap carries water and minerals throughout plants.

serotinous: releasing seeds in response to an environmental trigger, such as fire

sessile: attached, unmoving

species: a basic unit of biological classification for plants and animals. Members of the same species have a set of common characteristics that make them different from other life-forms. They are also able to breed with one another.

sperm: in plants, male reproductive cells produced in pollen. When sperm from pollen fertilize eggs (female sex cells) in ovules, the ovules grow into seeds.

symbiosis: a close and often long-term interaction between two organisms of different species, each benefiting from the interaction

taproot: the main root extending down from the plant stem

temperate climate: a climate without extreme temperatures or extreme amounts of precipitation

thermogenesis: a process by which living things create their own heat. Some plants use thermogenesis to attract insects, to warm fruit so that it expels its seeds, or to warm up the surrounding soil to allow seeds to grow.

thigmonasty: movement in plants triggered by touch. The closing of a Venus flytrap's leaves to capture an insect or the drooping of the sensitive plant's leaves when touched are examples of thigmonasty.

transpiration: the passage of water from a plant's leaves into the air

Vavilovian mimicry: a form of mimicry in the plant world in which a weed mimics one or more characteristics of a nearby domesticated plant

water vapor: water in gas form

SELECTED BIBLIOGRAPHY

Attenborough, David. *The Private Lives of Plants*. Princeton, NJ: Princeton University Press, 1995.

Blizard, Clifford. "Why Do Leaves Have So Many Shapes?" *Examiner*, May 8, 2010. http://www .examiner.com/article/why-do-leaves-have-so-many-shapes.

Capon, Brian. *Plant Survival: Adapting to a Hostile World*. Portland, OR: Timber, 1994.

Dietle, David. "10 Creepy Plants That Shouldn't Exist." *Cracked*, January 27, 2011. http://www .cracked.com/article_18979_10-creepy-plants-that-shouldnt-exist.html.

Foster, Bethney. "Facts on Opossums Playing Dead." Mom.me. Accessed April 1, 2016. http:// animals.mom.me/opossums-playing-dead-5274.html.

Geiling, Natasha. "Step Inside the World's Most Dangerous Garden (If You Dare)." *Smithsonian. com*, September 22, 2014. http://www.smithsonianmag.com/travel/step-inside-worlds -most-dangerous-garden-if-you-dare-180952635/?no-ist.

Hallock, Thomas, and Nancy E. Hoffmann, eds. *William Bartram, The Search for Nature's Design: Selected Art, Letters, and Unpublished Writings*. Athens: University of Georgia Press, 2010.

Heffernan, Sean. "Poems and Songs about Plants." *Ambius.com* (blog), December 31, 2014. http://www.ambius.com/blog/poems-and-songs-about-plants/.

Hugo, Nancy Ross. *Seeing Trees: Discover the Extraordinary Secrets of Everyday Trees*. Portland, OR: Timber, 2011.

Johnson, Steve. "Winter Shriveling." Cactiguide.com, December 22, 2013. http://www .cactiguide.com/forum/viewtopic.php?f=2&t=32237.

Kratz, René Fester. *Botany for Dummies*. Hoboken, NJ: John Wiley & Sons, 2011.

"Laws and Regulations." National Plant Board. Accessed April 1, 2016. http:// nationalplantboard.org/laws-and-regulations/.

Leitten, Rebecca Rose. "Plant Myths and Legends." Cornell University. Accessed April 1, 2016. http://bhort.bh.cornell.edu/conservatory/cpage3.html.

"Lichens." Offwell Woodland & Wildlife Trust. Accessed April 1, 2016. http://www .countrysideinfo.co.uk/fungi/lichens.htm.

Mathews, Kevin. "10 Incredible Plant Facts You Didn't Know." *EcoWatch*, December 31, 2013. http://ecowatch.com/2013/12/31/10-incredible-plant-facts/.

Pakenham, Thomas. *Remarkable Trees of the World*. New York: W. W. Norton, 2002.

"Plant Growth Factors: Photosynthesis, Respiration, and Transpiration." Colorado State University Extension. Last modified January 14, 2016. http://www.ext.colostate.edu/mg /gardennotes/141.html.

"Plants That Need Fire to Survive." *CreationRevolution.com*, June 29, 2012. http:// creationrevolution.com/plants-that-need-fire-to-survive/.

"Respiration in Plants." *BBC*. Accessed April 1, 2016. http://www.bbc.co.uk/bitesize/ks3 /science/organisms_behaviour_health/food_chains/revision/4/.

Richardson, Gillian. *10 Plants That Shook the World*. New York: Annick, 2013.

"So These Actually Exist: Flowers That Look Like Something Else." MetaPicture, June 16, 2013. http://themetapicture.com/so-these-actually-exist-flowers-that-look-like-something-else/.

Talalaj, S., D. Talalaj, and J. Talalaj. *The Strangest Plants in the World*. Melbourne: Hill of Content, 1991.

FURTHER INFORMATION

BOOKS

Baily, Tim, and Stewart McPherson. *Dionaea: The Venus's Flytrap*. Dorset, UK: Redfern Natural History Productions, 2013.

Buchmann, Stephen. *The Reason for Flowers: Their History, Culture, Biology, and How They Change Our Lives*. New York: Scribner, 2015.

Chalker-Scott, Linda. *How Plants Work: The Science behind the Amazing Things Plants Do*. Portland, OR: Timber, 2015.

Chamovitz, Daniel. *What a Plant Knows: A Field Guide to the Senses*. New York: Scientific American/Farrar, Straus and Giroux, 2012.

D'Amato, Peter. *The Savage Garden: Cultivating Carnivorous Plants*. Rev. ed. Berkeley, CA: Ten Speed, 2013.

Hughes, Meredith Sayles. *Plants vs. Meats: The Health, History, and Ethics of What We Eat*. Minneapolis: Twenty-First Century Books, 2016.

Jahren, Hope. *Lab Girl*. New York: Alfred A. Knopf, 2016.

Largo, Michael. *The Big, Bad Book of Botany: The World's Most Fascinating Flora*. New York: William Morrow Paperbacks, 2014.

Pollan, Michael. *The Botany of Desire: A Plant's-Eye View of the World*. New York: Random House, 2002.

Stewart, Amy. *Wicked Plants: The Weed That Killed Lincoln's Mother and Other Botanical Atrocities*. Chapel Hill, NC: Algonquin Books, 2009.

Trewavas, Anthony. *Plant Behaviour and Intelligence*. Oxford: Oxford University Press, 2014.

Wohlleben, Peter. *The Hidden Life of Trees: What They Feel, How They Communicate; Discoveries from a Secret World*. Vancouver, BC: Greystone Books, 2016.

WEBSITES

Alnwick Garden: The Poison Garden
http://www.alnwickgarden.com/explore/whats-here/the-poison-garden
Alnwick Garden in England grows the most dangerous and deadly plants on Earth. The website offers an introduction to the garden.

International Carnivorous Plant Society

http://www.carnivorousplants.org/cp/WhatAreCPs.php
Lovers of carnivorous plants have created an association. This website offers botanical information about these plants.

Lithops

http://www.lithops.info/en/index.html
This website is devoted to plants of the genus *Lithops*, also known as flowering stones and living stones. Here you'll find information about how to grow these plants, photos, and links to more resources to learn more about the plant.

Parasitic Plants

http://botany.org/Parasitic_Plants/
Learn about plants that live off of other plants at this website from the Botanical Society of America.

Smithsonian Gardens Orchid Collection

http://gardens.si.edu/collections-research/orchid-collection.html
Several species of orchids have evolved to resemble the insects they want and need to attract for pollination. You can explore these amazing and beautiful flowers at this website from the Smithsonian Institution.

FILM AND VIDEOS

Carnivorous Nepenthes Pitcher Plant
https://www.youtube.com/watch?v=6bexB8kAfXE
https://www.youtube.com/watch?v=B91njbu3ZOY
In these YouTube videos, horticulturist Brad Taylor shows the trapping and digestive process of pitcher plants.

"Flesh Eaters: Carnivorous Plants Lure Insects into Their Deadly Clutches"
https://www.youtube.com/watch?v=MnY_cCRELvs
In this YouTube video from Barcroft TV, insectivorous plants are shown capturing their prey.

Mimosa pudica
https://www.youtube.com/watch?v=BLTcVNyOhUc
The dramatic thigmonastic responses of plants are demonstrated in this YouTube video.

Squirting Cucumbers
http://www.arkive.org/squirting-cucumber/ecballium-elaterium/video-00.html
You'll witness the explosive seed dispersal of this cucumber in this video from Wildscreen Arkive.

What Plants Talk About. DVD. Arlington, VA: PBS, 2013.
In this video from the Public Broadcasting Service's *Nature* series, you'll learn from plant ecologist J. C. Cahill how plants communicate with one another in their effort to acquire vital resources, reproduce, and protect themselves from predators.

INDEX

SOURCE NOTES

7   "The Theme of Evolution in Plant Biology," Shmoop University, accessed June 24, 2016, http://www.shmoop.com/plant-biology/theme-a.html.

41   Natasha Umer, "Touching the Gympie Gympie Plant Will Make You Feel Like You're Being Electrocuted," *Upvoted*, November 14, 2015, https://upvoted .com/2015/11/14/touching-the-gympie-gympie -plant-will-make-you-feel-like-youre-being -electrocuted/.

69   Charles Darwin, quoted in Daniel Chamovitz, *What a Plant Knows: A Field Guide to the Senses*. (New York: Scientific American/Farrar, Straus and Giroux, 2012), 12.

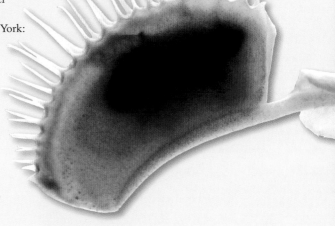

PHOTO ACKNOWLEDGMENTS

The images in this book are used with the permission of: © iStockphoto.com/Ekaterina Fribus, pp. 1, 95; © iStockphoto.com/Amy Riley, pp. 2, 86, 89; © Tim Gainey/Alamy, p. 5; © Kenny Williamson/Alamy, p. 6; © Laura Westlund/Independent Picture Service, pp. 8, 12, 16, 17; © iStockphoto.com/ooyoo, p. 10; © Rachel Carbonell/Alamy, p. 11; © Steve Hopkin/The Image Bank/Getty Images, p. 13; © David Curtis/Alamy, p. 17; Courtesy of the author, p. 19; © In Pictures Ltd./Corbis/Getty Images, p. 21; © John Plant/Alamy, p. 22; © Gerrit van Ommering/Minden Pictures, p. 26; © Neil Lucas/Minden Pictures, p. 27; © Rafael Ben-Ari/Alamy, p. 29; © Chien Lee/Minden Pictures, p. 31; © MYN/John Tiddy/Minden Pictures, p. 32; © Jogchum Reitsma/Minden Pictures, p. 33; © Bob Gibbons/Minden Pictures, p. 35; © David Cheshire/Alamy, p. 37; © Rick Strange/Alamy, p. 39; © SuperStock, pp. 42, 50; © Scott Leslie/Minden Pictures, p. 43; © Gianpiero Ferrari/Minden Pictures, p. 45; © Steffen Hauser/botanikfoto/Alamy, p. 46; © Science Photo Library/Alamy, p. 47; © Buiten-Beeld/Alamy, p. 49; © iStockphoto.com/istock-dk, p. 51; © Krystyna Szulecka/Minden Pictures, p. 51; © blickwinkel/Alamy, p. 52 (all); © Louise Murray/Visuals Unlimited, Inc., p. 55; © Jeff Mondragon/Alamy, p. 56; © epa european pressphoto agency b.v./Alamy, p. 57; © giuseppe masc/Alamy, p. 58; © Don Johnston/All Canada Photos/Getty Images, p. 63; © Tierfotoagentur/Alamy, p. 64; © Cisca Castelijns/Minden Pictures, p. 66; © Organica/Alamy, p. 67; © Louise Heusinkveld/Alamy, p. 69; © Sswartz/Dreamstime.com, p. 71; © Danita Delimont/Alamy, p. 73 (top); © State of Minnesota, Department of Natural Resources, p. 73 (bottom); © ETrayne04/Alamy, p. 75; © Todd Strand/Independent Picture Service, p. 77; © Jonas Gratzer/LightRocke/Getty Images, p. 79; © iStockphoto.com/JulianneGentry, p. 80; © Wendy Stone/Corbis/Getty Images, p. 83; Courtesy The Happy Organization/Photo by: Rosalinda Rachel Photography, p. 84;

Front cover: © Albert Lleal/Minden Pictures.

Back cover and jacket flap: © iStockphoto.com/Ekaterina Fribus.

ABOUT THE AUTHOR

Wiley Blevins is an author living in New York City. In addition to writing nonfiction for teens and younger readers, Blevins writes fiction, books for teachers on early reading practices, and textbooks for elementary schools. He also travels extensively throughout the United States, Asia, South America, and the Middle East.